TORAH,
LIGHT
AND
HEALING

TORAH, LIGHT AND HEALING

Mystical Insights into Healing
based on the Hebrew Language

Matityahu Glazerson

JASON ARONSON INC.
Northvale, New Jersey
London

First Jason Aronson Inc. edition—1996

Library of Congress Cataloging-in-Publication Data

Glazerson, Matityahu.
  Torah, light and healing : mystical insights into healing based on
Hebrew language / Matityahu Glazerson.
    p. cm.
  Previously published: Jerusalem : Lev Eliahu Leonard Himelsein
Foundation, 1993.
  Includes bibliographical references and index.
  ISBN 1-56821-934-2 (alk. paper)
  1. Jews—Medicine. 2. Gematria. 3. Medicine, Magic, mystic, and
spagiric. I. Title.
  BM538.H43G58   1996
  296.1'6—dc20   95-50733

Manufactured in the United States of America. Jason Aronson Inc. offers books and cassettes. For information and catalog write to Jason Aronson Inc., 230 Livingston Street, Northvale, New Jersey 07647.

DEDICATION

This book is dedicated to Myriam bat Moshe and Leon (Levi Yitzhak ben Elhanan haLevi) Tenembaum by their children and grandchildren. None of this would have been possible without their untiring devotion to their family and children, teaching us the lessons of chesed, tzdakah, and love for Judaism. We are forever grateful and this is a small expression of our appreciation and admiration. May Hashem bless them and us with many long years of health and unity.

With all our love,

**Gabriel, Michele, Elhanan Aryeh,
Avraham Meir, Yosef Simcha
and Adin Matityahu Tenembaum**

Agoura, California
Kislev, 5754

APPROBATION

to the author's work,
Sparks of the Holy Tongue
Rabbi B.M. Casper, z"l,
late Chief Rabbi of South Africa

*Rabbi Glazerson has broken new ground in the field of Jewish Religious Study by the original approach he has adopted in his book **Sparks of the Holy Tongue**.*

Delving into Jewish sources, he has managed to present a wealth of meaning and double meanings in the Hebrew Bible, in each case discovering and stressing a lesson of religious import.

The thoughts are presented in a straight-forward English and often are directly related to modern problems and happenings. In this way they have had an appeal to the minds of many students who have hitherto not had the opportunity of coming into contact with Jewish studies.

The book is a modest but useful contribution in this field.

———————————

APPROBATION

to the author's work,
Sparks of the Holy Tongue
Rabbi J. Salzer, z"l,
Rabbi of Adath Jeshurun Congregation,
Johannesburg, South Africa

Rabbi Matityahu Glazerson has rendered a great service to the Jewish public with the publication of his book. It gives the English reader the opportunity to delve into authentic Torah. Rabbi Glazerson disproves the tale that it makes no difference in which translation or language you happen to read the "Bible". He demonstrates that the Hebrew language possesses certain values which you hardly find elsewhere: a simple word expresses, in fact, deep ideas which the real meaning of the word includes.

The Torah is not reading material for leisure, but needs much effort in order to be able to penetrate its real meaning and discover its real beauty beneath the surface.

This book, which Rabbi Glazerson presents to us, is very topical today, when many thousands are searching for real values in a world of vanity. He teaches us to reach out for the eternal values which are to be found in our world when things are looked at from a proper perspective.

You find in the Hebrew language a new face; you find, in our much secularized world, eternal values. That is only one purpose of this publication.

CONTENTS

preface

TORAH AND SCIENCE

Torah is an internally consistent, self-contained thought system.

The scientific method is real. Scientists can competently diagnose, prognosticate, collect data, formulate hypotheses, test, etc., yet in the end science is forced to nullify itself through its inability to explain the **why.** For the pathologist, disease is probability – an actuarial exercise in genetic predispositions triggered by environmental factors, behavioral patterns, and the like.

The editor: ***Mordechai Rosner***

INTRODUCTION

An interesting set of circumstances, revealing the guiding hand of Providence, led to the writing of this book. While travelling and lecturing, the author came to Agoura Hills, California (near Los Angeles), where he gave a lecture after the conclusion of Shabbat (**Melave Malka**). The function took place at the home of Dr. Gabriel Tenembaum, a young gynecologist who had found his way back to Judaism and had become very involved in helping others on the same path. Dr. Tenembaum does not miss any opportunity to speak with people on this subject. Knowing the author's work and realizing its importance and potential for bring Jews back to their source, Dr. Tenembaum and his friend Mr. Zev Palmour (an Israeli who is also very involved in this field) approached the author, telling him about the extensive outreach activities of their community. They expressed their wish to be able to do more and more in this direction.

Dr. Tenembaum then asked the author to write a book that would enlighten the public on the topic of healing as viewed through a deep understanding of the

Hebrew language and the Torah and Talmud. He wished to dedicate such a work to his parents in appreciation for their help and support in his medical studies. For this purpose Dr. Tenembaum gave a generous contribution to enable the author to produce this work, which is now presented to the public.

The author would like to thank Dr. Tenembaum and Mr. Zev Palmour for their blessed initiative towards this goal. May the Creator bless them and their families in all their efforts both spiritually and materially, and keep them in good health.

At this opportunity the author would like to thank R. Shlomo Fox-Ashrei, a well-known translator, and R. Mordecai Rosner, an accomplished editor, who gave much time and effort to put the material, which is very complicated, into presentable form.

The author hopes that the insights shared here will shed light and, with G-d's blessing, open a new perspective on the vital topic of health, through deep insight into the Hebrew letters with which G-d created man.

This book is the latest building-block in the author's edifice of works on the profundities of the Hebrew language.

ABOUT THIS WORK

The aim of this book is to shed new light on the topic of healing as seen through the Hebrew letters. According to the Sages of the revealed and hidden Torah, these letters are the fundamental elements with which G-d created the entire universe, including man.

This connection can be seen through the fact that, originally, when a Jew was sick he did not need to go to doctors. Instead, through introspection and self-examination to discover in what way he had failed to fulfill G-d's commandments, he would know the source of his illness and how to remedy it. It was only later on, when man's spiritual state deteriorated to a more materialistic level, that "the doctor was given permission to heal," so that now man is not only allowed, but in fact commanded, to use medicines and medical techniques to cure illness. In later times, only certain individuals on a very high spiritual level were known to overcome illness through the original method. It is related, for example, that the brother of the Gaon of Vilna managed to cure himself in this manner without seeing a doctor.

Even today, though we rely on doctors, we need to

realize that only through G-d's help can the doctor's cure be effective, as we pray three times each day in the **Shemoneh-Esreh** (Eighteen Benedictions): "Heal us, and we shall be healed" (רפאנו ונרפא).

The doctor, too, needs this awareness. The Talmud says: "The good doctors go to Gehinnom (Purgatory)" (טוב שברופאים לגהנם). Some commentators point out that the numerical value of "good" (טוב) is seventeen. This refers to the Eighteen Benedictions, minus one — i.e., the request for healing. If the doctor considers himself "good," and thinks that he does not need to request that the cure should come from G-d, then he is one of the "good" doctors whose destiny is spelled out by the Talmud. This idea is reflected in the Hebrew letters. The letters א and ע belong to the same phonetic group, both being produced in the larynx. However, the א is a more refined, ethereal, "spiritual" sound; in fact its sound is not audible at all, while the sound of ע is coarser, more materialistic and earthy. Thus אור, **light,** which is the essence of existence, becomes on a more physical level עור, meaning **hide** or **skin,** the tough outer covering of animals and man. Simililary, פאר, the root meaning **splendor, beauty,** and connoting a harmonious, balanced connection between opposites, is spelled with א. But פער, spelled with ע, is a gross opening or **gap,** where the opposites are too far from each other and there is a break in continuity.

According to the Kabbalah, the transition from the purity of אור, **light,** to the materiality of עור, **hide,** came about through sin. The word for **sin** is חטא, which can be analyzed as א חט. The first part, חט, means to **dig,** or in reverse order, טח, **to plaster over, cover.** The second part, א, represents the Divine. Thus sin has a destructive effect on the divine element in man, causing it to be covered over with a thick materialistic **hide.**

These concepts are also reflected in the numerical value of the letters א and ע. The letter א, whose numerical value is 1, represents the pure unity of the Divine. The ע, numerical value 70, represents the expansion of this original unity into many details, as a single ray of light is refracted into a full spectrum of colors; for example, after his fall, Adam, who was one, became expanded into the Seventy Nations.

The rectification of this process is the spiritual history of man from the original sin until the final Redemption. The goal is to refine the material side of life (ע) and bring it back to the original situation when the א, the light of the Divine, shines unobstructed and pure. At that time, according to the Kabbalah, the letters of the Hebrew alphabet will again be manifested with their full light, revealing the true essence of Creation and man.

May this book, please G-d, be a humble contribution towards that goal.

Matitiyahu Glazerson
10 Kislev, 5754

Preface

from LETTERS OF FIRE

The purpose of this book, *Letters of Fire*, is to open a window for the reader onto the wondrous world, bathed in splendor and beauty, which lies concealed within the letters and words of Hebrew, the Holy Tongue. The deeper significance of the letters and words is discussed extensively in the literature of the Kabbalah. It is a subject as wide as all Creation. Every single letter points to a separate path by which the effluence of the Divine creative force reaches the various *sefirot** (ספירות, "spheres") through which the Creator, Blessed is He, created His world.

These matters, and the wonderful world they reveal, can remain a locked secret to which the ordinary person, unversed in Kabbalistic knowledge, has no access. The Sages of Israel, in their commentaries on the Torah through-

---

*The Kabbalah teaches that the primal impulse of Divine creative force reaches the world through an orderly progression of ten successive stages. Each of these, a world in itself, is called a *sefirah* (plural, *sefirot*). The Kabbalah assigns a name to each *sefirah*, divides the *sefirot* into various groupings, and explains their meaning and interrelationship. The present work makes no attempt to teach Kabbalah. However, I shall attempt to indicate the meaning of various Kabbalistic terms as they are needed for understanding the inner significance of the Holy Tongue.

out the generations, have revealed precious pearls from this wondrous storehouse of treasures. Thus they made it possible, even for those with no expertise in Kabbalah, to perceive the existence of this world. I too have drawn from this store of knowledge regarding the varied significance of the Hebrew letters and words. The sources are indicated throughout this work; in those instances in which a specific reference is not given, most are insights of our great scholars which I have read on various occasions.

The idea of writing this book came to me when I became aware of the exalted treasure trove of insights which are scattered among the writings of the medieval and later commentators (*Rishonim* and *Acharonim*), offering glimpses into the hidden world of the Holy Tongue. The material presented here contains fundamental ethical teachings from our holy Torah. The book is written in simple language which can be appreciated by every reader, even though the topics themselves are of the most exalted kind.

I wish to express my praise and thanks to *Hashem*, Who has enabled me to extract these precious pearls from the sea of Torah. May it be His will that their luster, shining forth, will draw hearts close to our holy Torah.

ON THE UNIQUE STATUS OF HEBREW, THE HOLY TONGUE

From *Pardes Rimonim, Sha'ar Ha-Otiot*, Chapter 1:

Many have supposed that the letters of the Hebrew alphabet are a matter of symbolic convention, that the Sages decided and agreed among themselves that certain signs would represent the sounds of speech. For example, they agreed that the sounds made by closing the lips would be represented by the forms of the letters: *beit* (ב), *vav* (ו), *mem* (מ), and *peh* (פ) — and likewise for the remaining sounds of the language. In the same way, other peoples also have symbolic representations for the sounds of their languages. According to this view, there is no difference between the Hebrew letters and the alphabets of other nations. The Hebrew letters are the conventional symbols used by the Israelite nation on the advice of Moshe through his prophetic inspiration, and the other alphabets are the conventional symbols of the other nations.

It follows, according to this theory, that the written words are nothing more than a means for making known the intent of the speaker. For example, a doctor who writes a book about the healing art doesn't intend that the book itself will be medicine; rather, he intends that the book should make known his thoughts or preferences on the subject of healing. Once the reader understands the principles of the healing art as written in the book, the book itself is of no intrinsic importance. Thus, if a person studies the book for years on end but does not succeed in learning the principles set forth therein, his study has done nothing for him and his soul has not been improved at all, since he still does not understand the requirements of the art. In fact, his study has actually done him harm, since he has wasted time and effort without gaining understanding.

The Torah, according to those who hold this view, is just like the medical textbook of our example; its purpose is to reveal the inner meanings and processes necessary for the perfection of the soul and if one does not master the required knowledge, he gains no benefit from his studies (God forbid).

This theory, however, cannot be true, for undoubtedly the words of Torah "restore the soul" (*Tehillim* 19:8). The proof is that the *Halachah* obligates us to read the weekly Torah portion, twice in the original Hebrew and once in the Aramaic translation, and this includes even seemingly meaningless place names such as Atarot and Divon (*Bemidbar* 32:3). This teaches us the perfection of the Torah: the very words and letters themselves have hidden inner meaning, spiritual power, and vitality.

From Chapter 2:

The letters of the Torah are not simply written according to agreed convention. Indeed, their form reflects the inner essence of their soul, for the shapes of these letters — the tiny extensions at their tips (*kotzim*), their "crowns" (*tagim*) and their component elements (*ziyunim*) — indicate definite spiritual concepts and supernal *sefirot*. The spiritual concept of each and every letter contains a glorious light, derived from the essence of the *sefirot*, which devolves [to this world] by stages, in accordance with the developmental order of the *sefirot*. Each letter is like a splendid palace, containing and corresponding to its spiritual concept.

When one of the letters is pronounced aloud, the corresponding spiritual force is necessarily evoked. Speaking Hebrew assumes holy forms which rise up and are sanctified at their root, which is the root of [the highest Kabbalistic world, known as] *Atzilut* (אצילות, "emanation"). These spiritual forces inhere not only in [the vocalized letters] but also in their written forms...

From the Words of Rabbi Tzadok Ha-Kohen
in his work, *Or Zarua La-Tzaddik*:

The Kabbalists, of blessed memory, the Sages of the Truth, taught that all the supernal worlds were created by combinations of the holy letters. And in this [lower] world, every created thing is kept alive by virtue of its name in the Holy Tongue. Therefore, the name which [Adam] gave to each thing (see *Bereshit* 2:19) is its true name. For example, the essential life-source of the שור (*shor*, "ox") is the force of the three letters ש, ו, and ר, in the upper worlds. It is the same for all earthly creatures and likewise for the created beings of all the worlds. Thus, every perceptive person will realize that it is fitting and excellent to call this language the "Holy Tongue" — for it is truly holy.

GUIDELINES TO GEMATRIA

To aid the reader in understanding the basic concepts of gematria employed in this book, some of the essential principles are summarized here.

1. Primary gematria: counting the numerical value of each letter

The thirty-two principles of exegesis used by the Sages to interpret the Torah are set forth in a *barayta* in the name of Rabbi Eliezer the son of Rabbi Yosei *Ha-Gelili*. The twenty-ninth principle is primary gematria. The commentary *Midrash Tannaim* states that the numerical values of the Hebrew letters were given to Israel at Mount Sinai. The values are as follows:

1 — א	10 — י	100 — ק
2 — ב	20 — כ	200 — ר
3 — ג	30 — ל	300 — ש
4 — ד	40 — מ	400 — ת
5 — ה	50 — נ	500 — ך
6 — ו	60 — ס	600 — ם
7 — ז	70 — ע	700 — ן
8 — ח	80 — פ	800 — ף
9 — ט	90 — צ	900 — ץ

The last five letters listed here (corresponding to the numbers 500-900) are the "final" forms of the letters כ, פ, צ, נ and מ, used when the letter comes at the end of a word. Sometimes these letters are assigned the same value as the regular form; for example, ך is counted as 20, just as is כ. But sometimes the "final" forms are used as shown above, to represent the multiples of one hundred, from 500 through 900.

2. Reduced gematria (gematria ketanah) or small numerical value (mispar katan)

The *mispar katan* is the primary gematria (see previous section) with any final zeroes removed. Thus, both 10 and 100 are counted as 1.

This type of gematria is basic to the teaching of *Tikkunei Zohar*, one of the basic works of Kabbalah. It is connected with what the Kabbalistic writings refer to as *Olam Ha-Asiyah*, the World of Action. This, the lowest of the worlds, is symbolized by the units, while the tens and hundreds symbolize the higher worlds. (See Ramchal, *Adir Ba-Marom*, p. 65.) Thus, when we reduce a word to its *mispar katan*, we discover how the concept represented by that word relates to *Olam Ha-Asiyah*.

Sometimes the primary gematria or the *mispar katan* is reduced even further by adding together all the digits of the number. For example, we saw above that the gematria of פרנסה is 395. This can ultimately be reduced to 8.

$$3+9+5 = 17$$
$$1+7 = 8$$

3. Full gematria: writing out the name of each letter

In this form of gematria, each letter of a word is written out in full, and the numerical value of all the resulting letters is counted. For example, by the full gematria, the value of קר is 696.

4. Interchangeability of letters which are formed in the same part of the mouth

Sefer Ha-Yetzirah, an ancient Kabbalistic work, states that the letters may be divided into five groups, based on the part of the mouth where the letter is produced.

1. אחה״ע. These are the guttural letters, formed in the throat, using the back of the tongue and/or the pharynx.
2. בומ״פ. These are the labial letters, formed primarily by closing the lips.
3. גכ״ק. These are the palatal letters, formed mainly by contact between the palate and the back third of the tongue.
4. דטלנ״ת. These letters are produced with the tip of the tongue against the front of the palate just behind the teeth.
5. זסשר״ץ. These are the sibilants, produced by expelling air between the teeth with the tongue held flat.

5. The Atbash (את בש) transformation

According to *Midrash Tannaim*, this type of equivalence was also given with the Torah on Mount Sinai. Therefore examples of it are found in the Talmud and Midrash. In the *Atbash* transformation, the first letter of the alphabet is interchangeable with the last, the second with the next-to-last, and so on. This results in the following table of equivalences.

א – ת	ד – ק	ז – ע
ב – שׁ	ה – צ	ח – ס
ג – ר	ו – פ	ט – נ
י – מ	כ – ל	

6. The Albam (אל בם) transformation

This type of equivalence was also given with the Torah at Mount Sinai, according to *Midrash Tannaim*. According to this transformation the letters of the alphabet are divided into two groups. The first letter of the first group is interchangeable with the first letter of the second group and so on.

א – ל	ה – ע	ט – ר
ב – מ	ו – פ	י – שׁ
ג – נ	ז – צ	כ – ת
ד – ס	ח – ק	

7. The Ayak-Bachar (איק בכר) transformation

According to the *Midrash Tannaim* the twenty-seven letters of the Hebrew alphabet are divided into three groups whereby each of the letters in the same group has the same small gematria. (The final letters are included in this transformation.)

א – י – ק	ד – מ – ת	ז – ע – ן
ב – כ – ר	ה – נ – ך	ח – פ – ף
ג – ל – שׁ	ו – ס – ם	ט – צ – ץ

8. The addition of the kollel

Sometimes, in finding the gematria of a word, we increase

the total by one. Rabbi Y. A. Chaver, in *Pitchei She'arim* (p. 252) explains that in such cases the root (*shoresh*) of a word is still attached to the upper world.

An example is the word ברית (*brit*, "covenant"). Its numerical equivalent, including the *kollel*, is 613.

ברית: 2+200+10+400 = 612

plus the *kollel*:   612+1 = 613

There are a total of 613 Scriptural *mitzvot*. Therefore we can say that this gematria teaches us that the concept of *brit* is attached and cleaves to the 613 *mitzvot*.

A related practice in gematria is to find the total numerical value of a word and then add the number of letters of the word. By this method, the word דגל (*degel*, "flag") has the numerical value of 40.

דגל: 4+3+30 = 37

plus the number of letters: 3+37 = 40

The Ba'al Ha-Turim finds a Scriptural basis for the practice of adding the *kollel* to a gematria. In the verse, "Efrayim and Menashe will be the same as Reuven and Shimon" (*Bereshit* 48:5), the words, "Efrayim, Menashe" have the numerical value of 726, while "Shimon, Reuven" have the numerical value of 725. Thus, when we add the *kollel* to the second pair of words, the values are equal. And the Torah itself testifies that they are "the same." This is a hint that sometimes it is necessary to add the *kollel*.

אפרים, מנשה:

1+80+200+10+40,+40+50+300+5   = 726

ראובן, שמעון:

200+1+6+2+50,+300+40+70+6+50   = 725

plus the *kollel*:   725+1 = 726

Rabbi Ya'akov Emden, in his commentary on *Pirkei Avot* entitled *Lechem Shamayim* sets forth (at the end of Chapter 3) basic principles for the use of gematria.

One cannot use gematria to introduce into the Torah innovations which are not confirmed by our early forefathers, who had direct and trustworthy traditions. However, one may use gematria to uphold the teachings of our Sages and the traditions of our forefathers, and whoever originates such gematria — his reward will be great. For this purpose, the scholar is allowed to search tirelessly for a gematria with which to support the words of truth.

It is in this spirit that the author of the current work has not only cited many instances of gematria and related exegeses from other authorities, but has also included some which do not appear elsewhere.

The Letters of the Alphabet as a Key to Understanding the Torah

Why is the Torah written without any indication of the beginning and the end of each verse, or of the proper vocalization of the words, i.e., without punctuation or vowels? *Rabbenu* Bachyei answers this question in *Chovot Ha-Levavot*. He says that this is in order to enable us to discover numerous and varied new meanings by punctuating and vocalizing the Torah in ways other than the standard ones, and by grouping the letters into new words, different from those which appear in our Torah scrolls. In this way, hidden worlds are opened and revealed to us. For example, Ramban writes in his commentary on the Torah that in the first words of the Torah: בראשית ברא, ("In the beginning [God] created"), the letters can be divided in a different way to read: ברא שיתברא ("It was created with [or for] the head"). This can add a new dimension to the understanding of the verse. An entire book has been written about all the possible combinations of the first word of the Torah, בראשית.

In this same light, the *Gaon* of Vilna explains the Gemara passage[1] dealing with the last eight verses of the Torah, in which the death of Moshe *Rabbenu* is described. The Gemara asks: How could Moshe *Rabbenu* have recorded his own death, which had not yet occurred? One of the answers suggested is that the Holy One, Blessed is He, dictated these verses to Moshe, "and Moshe wrote them with דמע (*dema*)." One possible meaning of the word דמע is "tears"; however, the Gaon says that this is not the correct interpretation. Rather, the meaning is "a mixture," as in the expression *terumah medama'at* (תרומה מדמעת), meaning sanctified food which has been "mixed" with ordinary food. That is to say, Moshe wrote the words describing his own death, but with the letters and words "mixed." Only after Moshe's death did Yehoshua discover that these letters, ordered differently, described the passing of Moshe.

This same idea can explain why the angels pressed their claim to *Hashem* that the Torah should be given to them rather than to the Jewish people.[2] At first glance, it would seem that the angels' claim is incomprehensible, since the laws of the Torah are relevant only to people of flesh and blood and not to Heavenly beings.

The answer, as the Sages tell us,[3] is that *Hashem* already had the Torah with Him, in the form of all of its letters, before He created the world. But the letters were combined into words only afterwards, forming the Torah as we know it. (This is similar to the process by which Yehoshua, after the event, reconstructed the verses describing Moshe's death.) The angels wanted the Torah to be given to them, but with the letters combined into words appropriate to their Heavenly nature.

The Hebrew letters help us to understand the Torah in other ways, too. In the introduction to his commentary on the Torah, Ramban lists the ways in which Moshe *Rabbenu* received the Torah from the mouth of the Almighty. These include: (1) the simple meaning, (2) hints and allusions,

(3) the numerical values of letters and words, and (4) teachings derived from the shapes of the letters, as well as other, similar methods. The *Tanna* Rabbi Eliezer, the son of Rabbi Yosei *Ha-Gelili*, lists thirty-two hermeneutic principles by which the Torah is expounded These include gematria (the numerical analysis of letters and words) and acrostics (joining the initials of words to form new words).

Let us consider, for example, the word לב (*lev*, "heart"), whose gematria is 32. Just as the heart is the source of life for the body, the thirty-two hermeneutic principles of Rabbi Eliezer are the heart of the Torah and through them we can receive the life that the Torah gives. The letters of לב are the first and last letters of the Torah: *Bereshit* begins with ב, and *Devarim* ends with ל. The letter ל represents למוד (*limmud*, "study"), as we shall see below. The letter ב represents "inner" meaning — its name is *beit* (בית, "house," "interior") which is found in the Torah in the expression "*within the curtain*" (מבית לפרכת).[4]

Ba'al Ha-Turim notes that these two letters, ב and ל, are the only two in the alphabet that can be combined with all the letters of *Hashem*'s name, י-ה-ו-ה, to make meaningful words: בי (*bi*, "in me"), בה (*bah*, "in her"), בו (*bo*, "in him"); לי (*li*, "to me"), לה (*lah*, "to her"), לו (*lo*, "to him"). None of the other letters have this feature: the letter מ, for example, can form meaningful words when combined with the letters י and ה, but not with ו. The significance of this observation is as follows: The heart (לב) is the point through which one can become completely connected to his Creator (י-ה-ו-ה). To this end, one must strive to make his heart pure and devoted to *Hashem*, thus achieving perfect attachment to Him.

The *Zohar* tells us that the Jewish people, the Torah and the Holy One, Blessed is He, are One.[5] Through the thirty-two (לב) hermeneutic principles, one becomes connected to the Torah, which is made up entirely of names of the Holy One, Blessed is He. The fact that the Torah is enclosed, as it were, by the letters of the word לב (*lev*, "heart") suggests to us that Torah study depends upon the heart of man, and also upon the thirty-two (לב) principles of interpretation. Why are these two letters found in reverse order, i.e. the ב at the beginning of the Torah and the ל at the end? This is to teach us that only through reviewing his studies, i.e. "going back" over them, can a person connect his heart to the Torah and come to know it through the thirty-two hermeneutic principles.

When read in reverse order, the word לב becomes בל (*bal*, "not"), indicating negation. One's life depends upon the heart; if one uses his heart properly, it can bring him to perfection. Otherwise, God forbid, it can bring him a feeling of lack and negation.[6] *Kohelet* says: "The heart of the wise man is to the right, and the heart of the fool is to the left."[7] That is, when we read the word from the right, לב (*lev*, "heart"), it shows the way of the wise; from the left, בל (*bal*, "not"), it shows the way of the fool.

chapter one

MAN'S APPROACH TO G-D

Man is a paradox!
Miraculous union of spiritual soul and physical body, man is the mortal, created being for whom the whole of Creation is brought forth. Bestowed with G-d-like intellectual and emotional powers, he treads the finite earth enjoined by heavenly decree. Man is at once the *"keeper of the garden"* and a cursed toiler for food. Searcher and dreamer, he is singular in his capability to change and be changed, to transcend the Here-Now and approach the Infinite One in Whose image he is made.

The medium for man's coming close is the Torah – G-d's will and wisdom as revealed to the people Yisrael

---

The keeper of the garden: ויקח ה' אלקים את האדם וינחהו בגן עדן לעבדה ולשמרה *(Genesis 2:15)*.

A toiler for food: ארורה האדמה בעבורך בעצבון תאכלנה כל ימי חייך *(Genesis 3:17)*.

Seventh Day, 6 Sivan 2448: The date of the Giving of the Torah, according to the calendar of the nations, was Saturday, June 6 in the year 1312 B.C.E.

on the Seventh Day, the sixth of **Sivan,** in the year 2448. For more than three millenia the Torah has been **the** consciousness of the Jewish nation and the focus of the most intensive analytical effort known to man. But the Torah is more than historical account and Divine directive, inspirational homily and holy writ; it is the Eternal Plan, the blueprint for Creation, the codework with which G-d has designed the spiritual and physical worlds and all they contain. Through the Torah, G-d has presented His Work to the Creation. Quite simply, the Torah is **the** Communication between Creator and all that is His.

To make the Divine Plan known and understood, the G-dly code Torah uses analogy, allegory, anthropo-morphism, arithmetic — all experiential, spatiotemporal terms the human mind may grasp. As the Torah itself states: *"Torah speaks in the language of man."* Through analysis of the Torah — its verses, words, and letters — the human mind can readily grasp the suprahuman logic

---

*Blueprint for Creation: See **Bereshit Rabba** 1:1 and **Zohar** 1:5a. The first verse of Torah states:*

בראשית ברא אלקים את השמים ואת הארץ:

"In the beginning G-d created the heavens and the earth."

Ostensibly, the Hebrew word את *is here the untranslatable grammatical device called the accusative; it "points its finger" at the definite-article prefix* ה *(the in English) that follows it. But commenting on one esoteric meaning of this profound first verse, the Kabbalist Rabbi Shimon bar Yochai, author of the **Zohar (Book***

contained therein. Through analysis of the Torah's component parts by such hallowed tools of exegesis as *gematria*, Hebrew-letter interchange, root-letter permutation, as well as through analysis of the Torah's system of internally consistent logic, it becomes clear to the searching student that all the secrets of Creation are included in the Torah, either explicitly or in hidden ways (see *Ramban: Introduction to the Book of Genesis*).

---

of Splendor), teaches that the word את is in fact here a shorthand code for the entire Hebrew alphabet (that is, the letters א through ת). Thus it is learned:

In the beginning G-d created . . .

[את: the twenty-two Hebrew letters

with which He then used to create]

. . . **the heavens and the earth.**

As taught in Kabbalah and Chassidut, the Hebrew letters are distinct conduits of the G-d ly lifeforce (emanations, life-force, influence — referred to metaphorically as **the G-d ly light**) that, in specific combination, actually detail the spiritual and physical composition of any worldly thing.

The Torah speaks: דברה תורה כלשון בני אדם *(**Berachot** 31b).*

Gematria: The numerical value of each Hebrew letter. The term in general refers to the method of Torah interpretation through the comparison of numerical values of Hebrew letters, words, and Scriptural verses.

chapter two

LIGHT

T
he most basic metaphor the Torah uses to describe G-dliness, G-dly emanations, indeed itself, is light, as is written: *"And Torah is light"* and *"Light is Torah."* Intangible yet of this world, light is un-

---

G-d liness . . . [the Torah] itself: Though it is impossible to speak about G-d 's essence (for such a level of understanding is beyond the ken of human intellect), one can learn about G-d 's emanations, referred to by the Torah as the G-d ly light. Indeed, the Torah as G-d 's will and wisdom are G-d 's first emanations. It is, quite simply, the way He most makes Himself known to man.

Light: In Hebrew, אור (*or*) and אורה (*orah*).

Light is a favorite metaphor of not only the Kabbalists but of the Talmudic and Midrashic Sages as well. See "The Light-Metaphor" in Jacob Immanuel Schochet's **Mystical Concepts of Chassidism,** Kehot Publication Society, Brooklyn, New York, 1979.

The Kabbalah favors the term אור because its numerical value equals that of רז (**raz**; secret, mystery):

אור: 1 + 6 + 200   = 207

רז: 200 + 7   = 207

To say that the Kabbalists and Sages favor the metaphor of light is to say that the Torah itself favors it. For the words of the bringers of Torah **are** Torah; all of the Torah was taught to Moshe (Moses)

ique in that it seemingly shares place in both the physical and spiritual realms. It is through the analogy of light that the human intellect can begin to perceive worlds more G-dly than our own.

The intrinsic connection between light and Torah is seen most clearly by means of the **At-Bash** transformation, in which the letter א correlates to the letter ת. Exchanging the א of אורה with ת produces תורה (Torah). Moreover, the **gematria** or numerical value of the plural form אורות (lights) is 613 – the number of Divine commandments (מצוות) as enumerated in the Written Law.

The English word **heal** is pronounced as is the Hebrew word הילה, which means **shining,** as in the verse: *"When His light was shining over my head."* Healing

---

even before it was revealed by those commentators and expounders who lived thousands of years after Moshe's death.

And Torah is light: ותורה אור (**Proverbs** 6:23).

Light is Torah: אורה זו תורה (**Megillah** 16b).

At-Bash (את-בש): Method of Torah interpretation by means of Hebrew letter interchange [the first letter (א) with the last (ת), the second (ב) with the penultimate (ש), and so on].

The gematria...of...אורות (lights):

אורות: 1 + 6 + 200 + 6 + 400 = 613

613: In Hebrew, תריג (**taryag**).

When His light: בהלו נרו עלי ראשי (**Job** 29:3)

The letters ה and ח: The guttural letters א,ח,ה,ע are produced by the throat, using the back of the tongue and/or the pharynx. Although grammarians include the letter ר in this group, the Kabbalah classifies it as a sibilant. See **Sefer Yetzirah.**

means restoring a person to the state in which his G-dly life-force shines forth as it should, a state in which he is able to both receive and emit the effulgence of Divine light.

Moreover, since they are both produced at the back of the throat, the letters ה and ח are interchangeable. When we exchange the ה of היל with ח, the result is חיל, meaning *strength* – another hint to the healing power of light.

In the Shabbat prayer *Yedid Nefesh,* we say:

> *Please G-d, please heal [my soul],*
> *please, by showing it the pleasantness*
> *of Your radiant light (זיוך).*
> *Then it will be strengthened and healed,*
> *and will have eternal joy.*

Here, too, we see the connection between light –

Interchangeable: Each of the twenty-two Hebrew letters may be classified according to its pronunciating source — that is, the five human organs of articulated speech from which the letters emanate: larnyx, lips, palate, tongue, and teeth. Those letters sharing a common source-organ may be interchanged for the purpose of Torah interpretation.

Yedid Nefesh: *ידיד נפש, "Beloved of [my] soul."*

Please G-d , please heal:

אנא א-ל-נא רפא נא לה

בהראות לה נעם זיוך

אז תתחזק ותתרפא

והיתה לה שמחת עולם

here referred to as זיו (*effulgence*) – and healing. Through the joy of perceiving G-d's brilliance, the soul is healed and strengthened.

Tellingly, the Hebrew word for darkness is חשך, the same letters spelling כחש, meaning *to be weak*. These are also the letters that spell שכח, meaning *to forget* – an unenlightening intellectual darkness promoting mental weakness for sure.

Sunlight has strong healing properties. The prophet Malachi states: "And you who fear My name, the sun of righteousness will shine for you, with healing in its rays." The Talmud cites two interpretations of this verse. According to Abbaye, this verse refers to the world as it exists today, before the coming of the **Mashiach** (Messiah). He says:

From this we learn that sunlight heals.

But R. Shimon ben Lakish disagrees. He maintains that the verse does not refer to our time, but to the Messianic era:

---

*The Prophet Malachi: (approx. 3622). "Malachi is Mordechai [the Jewish protagonist of the Purim miracle-story]." (**Megillah** 15a)*
And you who fear My name: וזרחה לכם יראי שמי שמש צדקה ומרפא
בכנפיה *(**Malachi** 3:20).*
*The Talmud cites: **Nedarim** 8b.*
Abbaye: The Talmudic sage Nachmani ben Kaylil (c. 4085).
Moshiach: (Lit., the Anointed One.) The Messiah.

> *There is no Gehinnom in the World-to-Come [the Messianic era]. Instead, the Holy One, Blessed is He, will take the sun out of its sheath [that is, its light and heat will be much more intense]. The righteous will be healed by it, and the wicked will be punished by it.*

Clearly, according to both opinions sunlight has the ability to heal.

The healing property that is now associated with the sun was originally in the possession of the Patriarch Avraham (see below, p.142).

It is taught that the name of the springtime month of Iyar (אייר) forms the initials of the verse, "I am G-d your Healer." It is in Iyar, the second month in the year

---

אייר: *From the Hebrew* אור *(light). See **Dictionary of the Targumim, the Talmud Babli and Yerushalmi, and the Midrashic Literature**, Marcus Jastrow, 1903, p. 47.*

I am G-d your Healer: אני ה' רפאך *(**Exodus** 15:26).*

Year of months: The Hebrew year is at once a solar and lunar system; its months are calculated according to the lunar cycle while the yearly pattern is amended and periodically intercalated to coordinate with the summer and winter solstices, thus keeping the Jewish festivals in their proper seasons.

*The year of months is stipulated by the first commandment of the Torah (**Exodus** 12:2); it is to begin with the first month called אביב (**Aviv**, spring), the time of the Exodus from Egypt — the month only later determined to be **Nisan** (ניסן). The year of festivals, interestingly, begins with **Tishrei**, the seventh month in the year of months, whose first day is called **Rosh HaShanah**, the "head of the year."*

of months, that the summer sun first begins to heal the earth from its cold winter weakness.

---

*States **Bnei Yissachar,** the Hebrew word אביב (spring) is itself an allusion to and a proof for **Nisan** being the first month. There, this word is read אב יב ("father of twelve"). That is, that the springtime month **Nisan** is the first ("the father") of the twelve months of the year.*

Winter: In Hebrew, חורף. This word can be interpreted as חי רף ("life is weakened"). The basic letters of חורף are חרף. When reversed, they spell פרח, which means "to flower." Winter is the reverse of flowering.

chapter three

SICKNESS

S ickness in Hebrew is חולי. This is related to the word חלל, which means *hollow* or *empty space,* and also to חול, meaning *secular* or *profane* – that is, empty of sacred content. Sickness is a state in which a person becomes void of light and spiritual content, with a resulting negative effect on his physical well-being.

The letter ח represents חומר (matter) and alludes to materialism, while the letter ל represents לימוד (learning) and לב (heart; see below, p. 142), an allusion to spirituality. The very shape of the letter ח depicts something closed off from the upper realms, while the ל, the tallest of all the letters, depicts man's ability to transcend the constraints of the physical world. In the root חל, which forms the basis of the words חול, חלל, and חולי, the ח precedes and dominates the ל. This indicates that in sickness as well as in the emptiness of secular life, the

---

חול: Note the similarity to the English **hollow.**

Sickness is a state: See ch. 31, **Igeret HaKodesh,** part 4 of **Tanya** of R. Schneur Zalman of Liadi.

All three of these words have the same **gematria:**

material aspect of living dominates and so burdens the spiritual.

Similarly, the word חלל also means one slain in battle. For the corpse is the most extreme example of the material overcoming the spiritual, so much so that the non-corporeal soul has fled the body, its physical abode.

The opposite of חלל is חיים (life) and חכם (wise, learned). All three of these words have the same *gematria* – an allusion to G-d's creation of everything in counterbalance to an equal, opposite thing. (Every letter of the Hebrew alphabet has its positive and negative aspect. Here the positive aspect of ח is חיים, life, while the negative is חטא, sin, and חומר, materialism.) The corpse (חלל) is counterbalanced by life (חיים) and wisdom (חכמה). Indeed, for the Jew, wisdom *is* life.

חיים: 8 + 10 + 10 + 40 = 68
חכם: 8 + 20 + 40 = 68
חלל: 8 + 30 + 30 = 68

G-d 's creation of everything in counterbalance: זה לעמת זה עשה האלקים *(Ecclesiastes 7:14).*

*Wisdom **is** life: In fact, G-d creates all life — indeed everything — with the **sefirah**-attribute of חכמה (**Chochmah, Wisdom**), as is written (**Psalms 104:24**): "How many are your works, G-d . You made them all with wisdom (**b'Chochmah**) and (**Proverbs 3:19**): "With wisdom (**b'Chochmah**) G-d founded the earth." And in the blessing following elimination: "You have created man **with** [that is, man is created through G-d 's **sefirah**-attribute of **Wisdom** as well as being himself imbued with the human intellectual faculty of] Wisdom* (אשר יצר את האדם בחכמה).

chapter four

ANNULLING SICKNESS

The root חלה which means *to be sick,* occurs (in various forms) five times in the Torah (*Genesis* 48:1, *Deuteronomy* 7:15, 28:59, 28:61, 29:21). The number five is important in several concepts having to do with the annulment of sickness, as we shall now explain.

Health depends upon achieving the proper balance between body and soul. Another way to express this is to say that one must find the proper balance between *material* (חומר) and *form* (צורה). Our body is the raw *material* while our soul, which is connected with the Divine, is the *form* which must mold and shape this material. The combined numerical value of these two words is 555.

חומר: $8 + 6 + 40 + 200 = 254$

צורה: $90 + 6 + 200 + 5 = \underline{301}$

$$555$$

The number five represents perfection or completion. For example, there are five parts of the soul (see below, p. 173) and five books of the Torah. Five is the numerical value of the letter ה, the letter with which the world was created. The number 555 consists of the number 5 in three positions: units, tens, and hundreds. These can be seen as three forms of matter, each of which, according to the **Arizal,** corresponds to one of the kabbalistic Worlds.

The units represent the solids, corresponding to the world of **Asiyah (Action)**; the tens represent the liquids, corresponding to the world of **Yetzirah (Formation)**; and the hundreds represent the gases, corresponding to the world of **Briah (Creation)**. Thus, the number 555 represents perfection on all three of these levels. In such a state of completion, where form and material (חומר and צורה) are properly combined, there is no sickness.

Thus the fact that the root **to be sick,** חלה, appears five times in the Torah, indicates that through Torah sickness is completely annulled from the entire Creation. The annulment of sickness depends upon living by the commandments of the Torah.

The number five also is identified with another strong force that nullifies sickness: the force of joy. The word **five** in its feminine form, חמש has the same letters as שמח, which means **happy,** while in its masculine form, חמשה it has the same letters as שמחה, **joy.** Happiness and joy banish sickness, as it is said: "A happy heart is good for healing" (לב שמח ייטיב גהה; **Proverbs** 17:22). We shall see below (p. 78) that the Patriarch Yaakov (Jacob) is particularly associated with healing.

Through the **Al-bam** (א-ל ב-מ) transformation (see Introduction), the letters of the name Yaakov (יעקב) transform to those of *joy* (שמחה):

י	becomes	ש
ע	becomes	ה
ק	becomes	ח
ב	becomes	מ

This is because Yaakov stands for perfection of the five parts of the soul (see below, p. 174, passage on **ohel**).

In the Hebrew alphabet, the letters following חל are טמ.

א ב ג ד ה ו ז **ח ט י** כ **ל מ** נ ס ע פ צ ק ר ש ת

The letters טמ form the basis of words meaning **blocked** or **obstructed**. Thus, טמטם means **stupidity,** a state in which intelligence is blocked; טמון, meaning **buried**; and טמיר, meaning **hidden.** Similarly, the word טמא indicates **spiritual contamination** or **impurity.** [Note that the word **contamination** is based on the root **tam,** which is homonymous with Hebrew טם, as in טמא, **contaminated.**] The same letters that spell טמא (*impure*) also spell אטם, a root meaning to block or seal. In this word, טמא, the letter א alludes to G-dliness and intelligence and is thus tellingly found at the end, under the domination of the letters טמ. Thus – טמ א – טמא can be interpreted as *"blockage of the Divine."* The close proximity of the combinations חל and טמ shows that sickness reflects both a physical and spiritual blockage.

The numerical value of the word חולה (**sick**) is 49.

חולה: 8 + 6 + 30 + 5 = 49

This equals the numerical value of the letters מט, a root that means **to collapse**. In reverse order they spell טמ. As just explained, these are the two basic letters of the word טמא, meaning **spiritually impure**. The Sages speak of forty-nine gates of impurity, and this is the numerical value of these two letters. Spiritual impurity leads to physical collapse. This is the inner meaning of the word חולה, **sick**. The remedy is through the twenty-seven letters of the Hebrew alphabet, which as mentioned above are **pure** (זך).

A powerful way of reaching a state of joy and purity is through music and song. According to the Kabbalah, the word שיר, which means **song,** comes from the word נשירה, meaning **falling away**; for song causes the confining shells (**klipot**) of materialism to fall away from the soul. [Compare Engl. **shear**, and see our work, **Music and Kabbalah.**]

Similarly, the word זמר, which means **song** or **melody,** comes from the same linguistic root as זמר, meaning to trim branches from a tree; for song has the power to cut away negative forces and remove the materialistic tendencies that tyrranize and oppress our souls. This is one reason why the **zemiros,** the Sabbath songs, are such an important part of that holy day. Music and song can open the soul and bring it to cleave to its divine source.

In this connection it is interesting to note that the Hebrew root meaning *to heal* – רפא – is similar to the English word *harp*. Thus the transliteration of ריפא, which means *he healed*, is *ripah*, which has the same consonants as harp. It is said that David played the harp to heal King Saul's spells of depression.

The word נגן, meaning *to make music,* is closely related to גהה, *healing,* for through the *Ik Bechar* (איק-בכר) transformation, נ (50) is equivalent to ה (5).

In our time, music therapy is a recognized method of healing.

Specifically, that the letters טמ immediately follow the letters חל indicates the process of disease: the profanation of human life through (חל) first causes a spriritual and then physiological blockage (טמ) of the G-dly effulgence (light) that vivifies all life, leading to spiritual and physiological disease (חולי). Similarly, the physical blockage is the cause of the spiritual blockage. Thus the Torah says in reference to forbidden foods: *"Do not contaminate yourselves and become contaminated*

Do not contaminate . . . through them: ולא תטמאו בהם ונטמתם בם *(Leviticus 11:43).*

The Sages comment: In the original, אל תקרי ונטמאתם אלא ונטמתם *(Yoma 39a).*

The commentators observe: See our work, **Letters of Fire**, ch. 5).

through them." The Sages comment: *"Do not read 'be-come contaminated' (ונטמאתם) but 'become obstructed"* (ונטמתם). The commentators observe that in exegeses of this type, the second reading (obstructed) indicates cause, while the first reading (contaminated) indicates effect.

Sometimes when we look at the letters of the alphabet that precede the letters of a certain word, we find the force that can annul that word. This is because the preceding letters are like the "roots" of the following one. By working on the "root," using it in a positive way, one can effect its offspring (see **Ben Ish Chai** to **Parashat Ki Tetze**). As we have seen, the basic root of the word **sickness** are the letters חל. The preceding letters in the alphabet are זך, a word meaning **pure, clear, clean,** as in the verse about the oil used in the Tabernacle candelabrum: *"pure olive oil"* (שמן זית זך; **Exodus** 27:20). Purity, clarity, and cleanliness annul the forces of disease. As we shall see below (p. 128), the word זך also refers to the Hebrew alphabet, for its numerical value is 27, the total number of letters in the alphabet. There it is explained that the alphabet is the spiritual basis of man's well-being.

The verb חלה means **became ill.** Here the letters חל, representing the non-sacred, precede and dominate the letter ה, which stands for G-d. Sickness ensues when the non-sacred side of one's life dominates and smothers one's connection with G-d.

— 47 —

We find a similar configuration in the word חלש, which means **weak**. Its final letter, ש, stands for learning and understanding, as in: *"You shall teach them [the words of Torah]"* (שננתם; **Deuteronomy** 6:7). The ש is dominated by the letters חל. Here we see hollow material interests dominating and pushing aside the learning of Torah, the outcome being **weakness.** In fact, the word חלש in Aramaic means the same as Hebrew חלה: **became ill.**

In Kabbalah the letter ה stands for the **sefirah-**attribute of **Binah (Understanding)**. Thus חלה, the root meaning to become ill, symbolizes a situation in which **Binah,** the power of thought and understanding, is suppressed. (For additional explanation of **Binah** as the source of health, see below, p. 61.) In Kabbalah the **sefirah-**attribute of **Binah** corresponds to hearing, or the ear. This shows the importance of the ear, hearing and understanding as a basis of health, as we shall see below in the section on *Torah and healing.* The word for **ear** is אזן, which is closely related to בחן, meaning **to analyze** or **to distinguish** one thing from another. Both words end in ן. The remaining two letters of בחן follow those of אזן in the alphabet.

ב	follows	א
ח	follows	ז

The letters of ear – אזן – are also the root of the word for **balance** (איזון). With understanding comes balance, which is the essence of health. (For more concerning the ear, see p. 154) In חלה, ***became sick,*** the ה, representing hearing, understanding, and balance, are suppressed and dominated by חל, the secular and materialistic.

Thus is the process of disease: Spiritual lack of light brings sickness, producing physical blockage. Physical blockage causes spiritual blockage which prevents the person from receiving his full allotment of G-dly light. To break this debilitating cycle, the doctor (רופא) must free the entrapped spiritual powers represented by the letter א (see below, p. 60).

Thus we see how the Hebrew language shows the essence of the concept it represents. For example, when we analyze the Hebrew word for ***sickness*** (חלה and related forms) we discover the inner meaning of the concept. By contrast, other languages represent only the surface meaning. The English word "disease," for example, tells us that the person is not at ease, but it does not reveal the underlying reasons.

chapter five

THE RESPLENDENT BALANCE

T he principal Hebrew root meaning *to heal* is רפא, as in רופא (physician, doctor, healer), רפואה (healing), From the letters of רפא is found פאר (resplendence), the shining beauty resulting from balance and harmony. The Arizal states that פאר is the spiritual source of healing. Health is a state in which all the necessary elements are in balance, resulting in a radiant beauty.

The root פאר can also be analyzed through its component parts: the letter פ represents the Hebrew word פה *(mouth* or *opening)* while the letters אר are the basic letters of אור, light. Thus the balanced spiritual

---

The Arizal: The Kabbalist R. Yitzchak Luria of Tzfat (1534-1572).

פאר *is . . . source of healing: See* **Kehilat Yaakov:** רפא.

Furthermore, the word פאר *is similar in sound to the English* **pair** *— a matching, balanced set. It is also similar to the English* **fair** *which, like the Hebrew* פאר, *has the double meaning of* **beauty** *("a fair maiden") and* **balance** *("a fair deal") and a connotation of light ("fair-haired" or "fair-skinned").*

The letter פ *represents [the mouth]: Seen sidewise, in its very shape.*

The opening of your mouth: פתח דבריך יאיר *(**Psalms** 119:130).*

state of פאר creates an opening for light, resulting in health. Indeed, this analysis of פאר hints to the importance of Torah-study for health. It is written: *"The opening of your mouth illuminates."* When a Jew speaks words of Torah, he in fact draws down and is enveloped by and imbued with the G-dly light that descends when G-d's will is fulfilled on earth. Thus Shmuel told his beloved disciple R. Yehudah:

> *Brilliant one, open your mouth [pro-nounce the words aloud] when you study Scripture; open your mouth when you study Mishnah.*

Balance is the basis of man's ***nefesh***, or soul. Thus the root שקל *(shakal)*, which means "to balance," has the same numerical value as נפש (nefesh). [Note the similarity between ***shakal*** and Engl. "scale."]

שקל: 300 + 100 + 30   = 430

נפש: 50 + 80 + 300   = 430

Likewise, the word פאר has the numerical value 430 when the names of its letters are written out in full and the "inner ***gematria***" (see Introduction) is taken. The names of the letters of פאר are:

פי	(*pei*)
אלף	(*alef*)
ריש	(*resh*)

Brilliant one: ***Eruvin 54a.***

Taking only the "inner" letters gives:

י	10
לף	110
יש	310
	430

This number, 430, is five times the numerical value of the word א-ל-ה-י-ם (*Elokim*), which means "G-d."

א-ל-ה-י-ם: $1 + 30 + 5 + 10 + 40 = 86$

$86 \times 5 = 430$

The number five represents the totality of physical space, i.e., the four directions plus the center. This is pictured in the letter ה, whose numerical value is five, and which consists of a ד (numerical value 4) with a י inside it, symbolizing the four directions with the point in the center. It also symbolizes the four elements (earth, air, fire and water), with the central י representing a fifth "element" (e.g., electromagnetic force) that gives energy to all four elements; on a higher level, the י represents the divine spark that gives life to everything created with the four elements. All this reveals other dimensions to the Sages' statement (*Menachot* 29b) that *"this world was created with the letter ה."*

We have just seen that the letter ה is composed of a ד with a י inside it. These two letters together spell יד,

which means **hand.** Thus the concept that *"this world was created with the letter* ה*"* also hints that G-d created the world with His hand, as it is written: *"My hand founded earth, and My right hand developed heaven"* (ידי יסדה ארץ וימיני טפחה שמים; *Isaiah* 48:13).

The numerical value of יד is 14, which hints at the fourteen joints of each hand – three on each finger and two on the thumb. All fourteen joints are included in the five fingers, just as the letters י-ד are included in the letter ה.

Since each hand (יד) has the numerical value 14, the two hands together have the numerical value of 28. This is the numerical value of the word כח, **strength.** Thus the creation of the universe with G-d's two hands is also hinted in the verse: *"The strength* (כח) *of His hands He told to His people"* (כח מעשיו הגיד לעמו; *Psalms* 111:10).

Creation with two "hands" is also hinted in the fact that the first verse of **Genesis** consists of twenty-eight letters. This verse contains seven words (corresponding to the seven days of Creation). The first three words contain fourteen letters (corresponding to one hand), and the remaining four words, fourteen letters (corresponding to the other hand).

The verse that immediately precedes the Ten Commandments likewise consists of seven words and twenty-eight letters. The first four words contain fourteen letters, and the remaining three words, fourteen letters.

— 53 —

This is a hint of the Sages' dictum that the world was created for the sake of the Torah, and on condition that Israel would accept the Torah (see **Rashi** to **Genesis** 1:1 and 1:31). It also hints that the Torah is the blueprint for Creation.

Thus the world was created with G-d's two "hands." The right hand represents the 248 positive commandments, and the left hand, the 365 negative commandments. As the Sages say: *"The right hand draws close and the left hand pushes away."* Adding together the digits of 248 (2 + 4 + 8) gives 14, and adding together the digits of 365 (3 + 6 + 5) likewise gives 14.

The Ten Commandments were written on two tablets of stone, five commandments on each tablet. This too is mirrored in the two hands, with five fingers on each hand.

The Ten Commandments are the root of the entire Torah. Thus the Ten Commandments contain 620 letters. There are 613 letters up to the last two words, corresponding to the 613 Scriptural commandments. The last two words, *"which belongs to your fellow"* (אשר לרעך; **Exodus** 20:14) contain seven more letters, corresponding to the seven Rabbinic commandments that complete the "Crown" of Torah (see below, p. 116), or to the seven Noachide commandments given to the other nations.

In all this we see again the principle that there is an intimate connection between our physical body and our spiritual body. *"Through my flesh I see G-d"* (see below, p. 103; and see p. 169, *The connection between soul and body*).

The number five is also signficant because there are five books in the written Torah, and five parts of the mouth that participate in making the sounds of speech (throat, palate, teeth, tongue, and lips). The very first word of the Torah, בראשית, is pronounced with all these five parts of the mouth, showing that the power of speech is the basis of all Creation.

When a person studies the five books of the Torah, and thereby becomes aware that the totality of the universe is filled with G-d (*Elokim*), and when he expresses this awareness through his speech, then his soul is in a state of balance (שקל) and harmonious splendor (פאר). This is the spiritual foundation of health.

Similarly, the word רפואה, meaning *healing,* is composed of the letters of the words אור (light) and פה (mouth). If one wishes to be healed, let him fill his mouth with the G-dly light.

This message is symbolized by the Candelabrum (*Menorah*) that stood in the Temple in Jerusalem. Its primary purpose was to give physical light. The Alshich teaches that its seven-branched form represents the human face. The two outermost branches (on the far right and the far left) correspond to the ears. The next two inner branches correspond to the eyes. The next two, the nostrils, and the central light, the mouth.

eye   ear   nostril   mouth   nostril   ear   eye

This, states Alshich, teaches that these most basic senses depend upon the faculty of speech. Furthermore, it illustrates the centrality of the power of speech to the health of the body: that the proper use of the mouth – in accordance with the Torah – is a central channel of light to vivify the entire body.

When the order of פאר is disrupted, the result is פרא, meaning **wild** or **uncontrolled** – a fitting description of the disordered state of poor health (cancer, for

Alshich: R. Moshe Alshich, maggid (preacher) and author of **Torat Moshe** on the Five Books of Moshe (**Parashat Terumah**).

example, is the uncontrolled proliferation of cells). The significance of פרא can be understood by analyzing the meaning and position of its letters:

א

The letter אלף‎(א, *alef*) represents the Holy One, Blessed is He, Who is the Leader (אלוף, *Aluf*) of the universe. The letter א also stands for *learning* or *intelligent thought,* as in the verse: "*I shall teach you* (ואאלפך) *wisdom.*" Thus, the א represents man's connection with G-d through his G-d-given intelligence, with which he learns to do G-d's will as stated in the Torah.

Moreover, the letter א also represents *faith* (אמונה, *emunah*), the Jew's supernal soul-power surpassing his intellect. Though it distinguishes man from the lower creations, the human intellect of reason is by nature limited; the intelligent brain can grasp only those realities as it can. Furthermore, intelligent though he may be, any man is endowed with so much intellect, and no

---

The Holy One . . . the Leader: ואין אלוף אלא הקב׳ה *(Chagigah 16a).*

אלוף: *Note the similarity to the English* **aloof,** *meaning* **distant, lofty, removed.**

I shall teach you wisdom: ואאלפך חכמה *(Job 33:33).*

more. Therefore, in order to reach to higher realms –
and there connect with the Source of All, the Supreme
Intellect – man must at times hone his higher, unlim-
ited soul-power called faith (אמונה).

Thus, א represents a Jew's connection with G-d:
first through intelligence and then through the more
sublime soul-power of אמונה.

פר

The remaining two letters of פרא are פר. These
letters stand for raw power, as in the word פר, meaning
bull, the most powerful of domesticated animals. [Note
the similarity in sound between English "power" and
Hebrew פר.]

Hone his ... faith: The Hebrew word אמונה *stems from the root* אמן,
meaning **artist** *or* **craftsman.** *Fittingly, each Jew must perfect his
art of faith through intensive concentration on and practice of Torah
values in all aspects of human life.*

*Soul-power called faith: Where intellect ends, faith begins. Today,
blinded by the spiritual darkness of the Exile, we are now — in the
moments just prior to the coming of the Moshiach –prevented from
witnessing the open revelations of G-d liness as did our ancestors.
What is more, our accumulated wisdom and intellect are no longer
given over to Torah scholarship but to the pursuit of secular, pro-
fessional studies. It is therefore the Jew's* **emunah** *in the One
Above that must necessarily be called upon to enlighten the Exile.
For just as a single spark can intensify into a brilliant beam of light,
so too can a flickering of faith —*אמונה *— spread forth to irradiate
this dark, physical world and illuminate G-d 's hidden ways.*

In the word פאר, the א (intelligence) is in the central position, where it balances power (פר) through its service to G-d (אלוף). In the word פרא, however, the letters פר are in the leading position, dominating the א. In this position, where animal brute strength dominates and subjugates the divinely directed intellect, health is overpowered and lost.

The solution is usually sought with the help of a doctor or healer (רופא). This word can be analyzed as רף, meaning to **loosen,** or **free**) plus the letter א. This indicates that the task of the healer is to liberate the א from the dominion of the פר, thus restoring פאר – the balanced state that brings health. If health cannot be restored and the element of raw power is let to run wild, what results is the disintegration of the body's elemental balance, resulting in אפר (ashes).

A related analysis of פר and פאר is given in the Talmud **Shabbat** (104a), which explains that the letter פ represents the mouth (פה), while ר represents the head (ראש). The combination פר, then, indicates a direct connection between head and mouth. [For sure, speech must always emanate from one's thought.] More specifically, the root פאר indicates the moderating influence of א – intellect – as it mediates between thought and speech. And such is a principal obligation of the Jew: to

---

פ. כפופה פ' פשוטה פה פתוח פה סתום :(Talmud **Shabbat** (104a

examine at all times the thoughts in his head (ר) in the light of G-d's intellect (א) as found in the Torah. Only then will he express his thoughts with his mouth (פ). The correct placement of the א is therefore crucial for balance and for spiritual, emotional, and even physical health.

◇ ◇ ◇
◇

chapter six

UNDERSTANDING AND HEALING

A nother word for health is צרי, which means *balsam,* a medicinal tree sap mentioned as a symbol of healing, as in the verse: *"Is there no balsam in Gilead; is there no doctor there?"* (הצרי אין בגלעד אם רפא אין שם; *Jeremiah* 8:22). The same three letters that spell צרי (*balsam*) also spell יצר (*yatzar – to produce, create*), which is the root of *yetzirah.* In Kabbalah existence is arranged in four "worlds" (*Atzilut, Briah, Yetzirah,* and *Asiyah*), of which the third, *Yetzirah,* corresponds to the *sefirah*-attribute of *Tiferet* (*Splendor*), which is especially associated with healing (see p. 78, sec. 11).

This word, צרי (*balsam*) is closely related to the name of the vowel, צירה (*tzereh*). In Kabbalah, the vowel *tzereh* is said to correspond to the *sefirah*-attribute of *Binah (Understanding). Binah* is the root of the seven lower qualities, because it is directly above them (it is the eighth from the end when the Tree of Life is constructed with *Keter* and without *Daat)*: These seven lower *sefirah*-attributes are: *Chessed* (*Kindness*), *Gevurah* (*Strictness*), *Tiferet* (*Splendor*),

— 61 —

Netzach (Eternity), *Hod (Glory)*, *Yesod (Foundation)*, and **Malchus (Kingship)**. As such, **Binah (Understanding)** is the root of healing; for health results from the full development and harmony of the seven *sefirah-*attributes. When understanding comes, healing follows, as it is said: *"Their heart will understand and they will repent and be healed"* (ולבבו יבין ושב ורפא לו; *Isaiah* 6:10).

The numerical value of the word בינה *(Binah, Understanding)* is 67. When 1 is added for the **kollel** (see Introduction), the total is 68, which is the numerical value of חיים, **life**. **Understanding** is the source of life. (See also p. 111, on the relationship between חכם, **wise,** and חיים, **life.**)

◇ ◇ ◇
◇

chapter seven

BRAIN AND HEART

The two principal centers of spiritual activity (thought and emotion) are the brain and heart. In the Kabbalah, the head corresponds to the brain, while the mouth corresponds to the heart. The Hebrew word for ***brain*** is מח, while the word for ***heart*** is לב. Together these constitute man's spiritual nature, known in Torah as the *"image of G-d"* (צלם אלקים; ***Genesis*** 1:27) in which man was created. The name of G-d the Torah uses here is אלקים (***Elokim***), the name of G-d describing His creation of and involvement in the physical world. In fact, the numerical value of the phrase מח ולב (brain and heart) is equal to that of אלקים.

Another linguistic root showing the proper connection between the brain and mouth is אלף. As we saw above (p. 60), this root indicates learning about the will

---

מוח ולב ...	*is equal to* ...	אלוקים:
מח ולב:	40 + 8 + 6 + 30 + 2	= 86
אלקים:	1 + 30 + 5 + 10 + 40	= 86

of G-d. Its three letters represent the three parts of the body:

א
___

The **א** represents the brain. The inarticulate **א** – translucent, luminous, aloof – is the first, most spiritual of the Hebrew letters. As such it corresponds to the human brain, the most spiritual organ of the human body and the primary dwelling place of the **neshamah,** the G-dly soul.

ל
___

The letter **ל** represents the heart (see below, p. 142, sec. 10a), and Torah learning; the **ל** is the initial letter of לב (heart) and לימוד (study).

פ
___

The letter (**פ**) represents the mouth. In the root אלף, the letter **ל** mediates between the **א** (brain) and **פ** (mouth). This indicates the path of thoughts entering the brain (**א**) and passing through a heart (**ל**) that has absorbed the teachings (**ל**) of Torah. Only afterwards do the thoughts proceed to the mouth (**פ**). But if the letter **ל** (the studious heart) is removed from אלף, what remains is אף (anger). Thoughts unchecked and allowed to pass directly from the brain to the mouth can result in anger.

Thus it is not surprising that the quality represented by א (intelligent learning of G-d's will) is the life essence of man and the world. If the א is removed from the word אדם (*man*), what remains is simply דם, the Hebrew word for *blood*. These letters also allude to the root composing the Hebrew words for *silent* (דום) and *inanimate* (דומם) – empty entities all of them.

In the word אדם (*man*), the א, as we have seen, stands for the Divine. The ד, whose numerical value is 4, represents the four elements from which man's physical body is made – earth, air, fire, and water. The letter ם (i.e. מ) has the numerical value 40, or 4 × 10. Multiplying by ten indicates that the concept is reflected on a higher level. In the present instance, the four elements on a higher level comprise man's spiritual body, i.e., his soul. Thus the word אדם shows the basic parts of which man is composed: the divine source (א), the physical body (ד), and the soul (ם).

This is further revealed in the word ולד, which means *fetus*. Its numerical value is 40. The Sages state that it takes forty days for the fetus to be completely formed in the womb. (For example, during the first forty days one may still pray that the fetus should be a boy or a girl.) Here too we find the concept of 4 × 10, the four

---

What remains is . . . blood: And blood is the "stuff of life" — of the mortal body, not the soul, as it is written: "For the life of the flesh is in the blood." כי נפש הבשר בדם היא (Leviticus 17:11).

The Hebrew word for . . . silent: Compare the English dumb.

physical elements of the world (4) reaching perfection (10) in the completed fetus.

Likewise man's spiritual sustenance is connected with the number 40. If he should become ritually contaminated he purifies himself by immersion in a *mikveh* (ritual bath) containing a minimum of 40 *s'ah* of water. The Torah, the spiritual basis of his life, was given to Moses during his forty days on Mount Sinai.

Similarly, when the א is removed from ארץ (earth) what remains is but רץ ("it runs"), a life-long marathon of motion devoid of higher purpose. [Note the similarity in sound between ארץ (*eretz)* and *earth.*] And most interestingly, without G-d's wisdom (א), the word אמת (truth) is truly lifeless indeed (מת, dead). So the Sages have said:

> *The wicked [that is, the unbelievers who refuse to learn G-d's wisdom and do His will] are in their lifetimes called dead (רשעים בחייהם נקראים מתים).*

These qualities represented by פאר are intrinsic to man's existence, to his very form and likeness. Therefore is the word תפארת (beauty), from the root פאר, used to express the *image of man*. In the Book of Yeshayahu,

---

What remains is but רץ: And as the author of **Sidduro shel Shabbat** points out, the same two letters reversed spell צר, meaning **narrow** — a hint to the root צרה, meaning **trouble**. Life

the Prophet speaks of the craftsman who fashions an idol *"like the form of a person, like the splendor* (כתפארת) *of man* (אדם)."

On a deeper level, the word פאר, as interpreted by the **Al-Bam** (אל-בם) transformation, equals 45 – the numerical value of the word אדם. More significantly, forty-five is the numerical value of the word מה (***What?***), an allusion to the *sefirah*-attribute חכמה (***Chochmah, Wisdom***) expressed as the innate intellectual faculty of the Jew (who is called אדם). Moreover, מה refers to the *sefirah*-attribute of תפארת and to the permutations of the Ineffable Name of G-d related to תפארת.

$$\diamond \ \diamond \ \diamond$$
$$\diamond$$

without the blessing of the א is a troubled one, for sure. Book of Yeshayahu: ויעשהו כתבנית איש כתפארת אדם *(44:13).*

Al-Bam *(אל-בם): Method of Torah interpretation by means of Hebrew letter interchange [the first letter (א) correlates to the twelfth (ל); the second (ב) to the thirteenth (מ); the third (ג) to the fourteenth (נ); and so on].*

The word פאר *. . . equals the numerical value of* אדם:

פ ... ו	= 6
א ... ל	= 30
ר ... ט	= 9
	45
אדם: 1 + 4 + 40	= 45

chapter eight

THOUGHT — THE ESSENCE OF MANS VITALITY

second Hebrew root for healing is גהה, as in the
verse: *"A happy heart is good for healing."* The
same letters in different order spell הגה,
meaning **to think** or **contemplate,** as in the verse: *"You
shall meditate (והגית) upon it [the Torah] day and night."*
These roots are closely related to the root נגה, which
means **shining with light,** as in the verse: *"Light will
shine (אֹ) on your paths."* Here again we see the close
relationship between healing, light, and spiritual full-
ness.

Another allusion to the spiritual source of healing is
made by dividing the letter ג of גהה into its component
parts. In a Torah scroll, the ג is written by combining

A happy heart: לב שמח ייטיב גהה *(Proverbs 17:22).*
You shall meditate: והגית בו יומם ולילה *(Joshua 1:8).*
Light will shine: ועל דרכיך נגה אור *(Job 22:28).*
*Component parts: See **Magen David** of the **Taz** [R. David Segal
(d. 5427)] which mentions this type of word analysis.*

the letters ' (*yud*) and ו (*vav*). (The ' forms the short leg of the ג.) Thus גהה can be deciphered as י-ה-ו-ה, the four-lettered, Ineffable Name of G-d.

The numerical value of גהה is thirteen, which is also the numerical value of the words אחד (one) and אהבה (love). This, too, shows that closeness to G-d is the source of healing; for oneness and love are attributes of G-d, and in fact the word אהבה forms a name of G-d.

The fact that the words גהה (*healing*), אחד (*one*) and אהבה (*love*) all have the same numerical value tells that the power of healing (גהה) is the ability to unify – to produce harmony among the component elements of the body, among the component elements of the soul, and between the body and soul.

Through the **Ik-Bechar** (איק-בכר) transformation, the letter ג corresponds to the letter ל. This means that הגה (thought) transforms to הלה, another form of the word הילה – *shining*. Thoughtfulness (הגה), then, can

---

The numerical value of גהה:

    גהה: *3 + 5 + 5*   *= 13*

    אחד: *1 + 8 + 4*   *= 13*

    אהבה: *1 + 5 + 2 + 5 = 13*

Ik-Bechar *(איק-בכר): Method of Torah interpretation by means of Hebrew letter interchange [the first letter (א) correlates to both the tenth (י) and the nineteenth (ק); the second (ב) to both the eleventh (כ) and the twentieth (ר), and so on]. Thus each letter corresponds*

illuminate a person's life with shining light (הילה) and thereby produce health (גהה).

R. Samson Raphael Hirsch states that since the ג and י are interchangeable as palatal letters, the word הגה transforms to היה (being). The spiritual power of man – his faculties of thought, comprehension, meditation, emotion – is the essence of his very being, and thus is essential to both his mental and physical health.

Again through the *Ik-Bechar* transformation, the letter ה is interchangeable with נ. Thus הגה is transformed to נגן (to make music). Not only does music have a joyous influence on one's thoughts, but melody can actually introduce a G-dly light into the soul and improves one's health.

Through two different methods of interpretation, both הגה (thought) and נגה (shining light) can be transformed into the word נקה (to clean). As mentioned above, the letters ג and ק are interchangeable as palatals.

---

to the other letter(s) whose numerical values are multiples of ten. For example, the numerical values of א-י-ק are 1-10-100.

R. Samson Raphael Hirsch: (**Parashat Vayera**).

[Music's] joyous influence: Music and its related wisdom mathematics are the two wholly pure secular pursuits. Through them man on earth glimpses the simple oneness and unity of G-d as revealed in the supernal worlds. Harmony and rhythmn, system and logic — the simple, universal human joy of the musical-mathematical experience is proof-positive that these disciplines are our gifts from Above.

Thus נגה becomes נקה. Moreover, R. Samson Raphael Hirsch indicates the connection between הגה and נקה as found in the verse: *"Remove (הגו) the dross from the silver, and a vessel emerges for the refiner."* The word הגו is a form of הגה meaning **to remove** impurity from silver. Likewise, one achieves spiritual and physical health by removing the impurities from one's thoughts (הגה).

Similarly, the root meaning **to remember,** זכר, can be analyzed as זכ, meaning **pure,** plus the letter ר **(reish, ריש)**, which stands for the **head (rosh, ראש)**. Good memory depends on purifying the mind. This is further clarified by the fact that these same three letters, זכר, when written in different order, form רכז, the root meaning **to concentrate.**

On a deeper level, the word כלי (vessel) in this verse alludes to כליון הנפש (yearning of soul) while the word כסף (silver) alludes to כיסופים (desires). Thus the verse hints to the potential for spiritual and physical health – to purge oneself of one's baser desires and

---

The ג and י: The palatal letters ק,כ,י,ג are formed primarily through contact between the back portion of the tongue with the palate.

Remove the dross . . . refiner: הגו סיגים מכסף ויצא לצרף כלי *(Proverbs 25:4).*

The numerical value of נקיון . . . יראה . . . גבורה:

נקיון: 50 + 100 + 10 + 6 + 50 = 216

יראה: 10 + 200 + 1 + 5 = 216

גבורה: 3 + 2 + 6 + 200 + 5 = 216

thereby transform oneself into a vessel fitting to receive G-d's more sublime bounties. Moreover, the numerical value of נקיון (*cleanliness*) is 216 – the numerical value of both יראה (fear of G-d) and גבורה (strength). When a person cleanses himself spiritually, he achieves fear of G-d as well as physical and emotional strength.

On the physical level, as on the spiritual, sickness causes a person to have distorted appetites (כיסופים). Bitter becomes sweet, tasteful food becomes bland, etc. When the body is cleansed, the appetites become orien-ted towards the right things.

chapter nine

THE HEALING POWER OF PEACE

P erhaps the most widely known of all Hebrew
words is שלום, the Hebrew word for *peace.* The
word שלום comes from the root שלם, meaning
whole or *complete.* After Yaakov's struggle with the
Angel, the Torah states: *"Yaakov came whole* (שלם)."

As does the root פאר (see above, p. 50, sec. 6), the
root שלם represents balance, moderation, and harmony.
According to **Sefer HaYetzirah (The Book of Formation,** a kabbalistic work attributed to our forefather
Abraham), the first letter of שלם, the letter ש, represents
fire (אש) while the last letter מ represents water (מים).
(Note that the shape of the ש resembles flames. And
note the similarity between the name of this letter, **shin,**
and English words such as "shine" and "sheen.") In the
word שלם, these two antithetical forces are balanced by
the ל representing the heart (לב). The form of the ל
reveals a central chamber with a vein entering and an
artery exiting. In the word לב, the ל is accompanied by

Yaakov came whole: ויבא יעקב שלם **(Bereshit** 33:18).

the letter ב, the letter whose name (בית) means *house* or *chamber* and whose numerical value is two. Thus the word לב itself vividly illustrates what is known — that the heart is a bifurcated chamber of blood-intake and - outflow. Moreover, the incoming venal blood is blue, the color of water. The outgoing arterial blood is red, the color of fire. Physiologically, too, the heart (ל) harmonizes the forces of fire and water.

When we write two of the letter ל facing each other (one drawn normally, with the curve to the right, and the other with the curve to the left), it makes a complete picture of the heart (R. Avraham Abulafia). Thus the root חלל, meaning *to desecrate,* shows the letter ח, which stands for the secular and profane, dominating the complete heart (לל).

The word שלום comprises the root שלם plus the letter ו. The ו is the Hebrew letter of connection. The name of the letter, *vav,* means *a hook* or *nail,* an implement that connects things. Its name in Hebrew is ואו, whose letters have the numerical value of thirteen. This is the numerical value of the word אחד, *one,* the word of unification. Linguistically, ו is the Hebrew conjunctive prefix (rendered as *and* in English). Graphically, it represents connection and, specifically, the connection that unites opposites. Its long, straight form indicates

---

House of Yaakov . . . Egypt: **Genesis** *46:27.*

union between the upper and lower worlds as well as the drawing down of the G-dly light into the physical World of Action in which we exist. Its numerical value is six. The **vav** represents both the six **sefirah**-attributes (**Chesed** to **Yesod**) as well as the sixth **sefirah**-attribute **Yesod,** the **sefirah**-attribute that unifies the upper and lower worlds. In Kabbalah, ו, the third letter of G-d's name (י-ה-ו-ה) corresponds to Yaakov, the third Patriarch. The name of the letter, ואו, is said to represent the twelve tribes, six on one side and six facing them, with Yaakov in the center unifying them. The ו at the beginning and end of the word has the numerical value of six, representing six tribes, while the central א has the numerical value of one, representing Yaakov, the unifier.

All said, the balance and harmony of שלם (and therefore of שלום) are of a lower, more earthly form than those of פאר. In פאר, the harmonizing element is א, which represents the higher, abstract intellect. In שלם, the harmonizing element is ל, which represents the emotions and desires, and the thoughts associated with them. Both types of harmony contribute to the state of good health.

The word שלום, **peace** has the same letters as מושל, which means a **ruler** or **governor.** This teaches that one who governs his own heart is a man of peace, bringing peace to himself and others.

The central letters of שלום are לו. As we have seen, ל represents the heart. The straight form of the ו represents honesty and directness. A straight, honest heart is a prerequisite for peace.

Another outcome of a straight, honest heart is *joy,* as it is written, *"The straight of heart have joy"* (וֹלישׁרי לב שׂמחה; *Psalms* 97:11). The word שׂמחה, *joy,* begins with שׂמ, the letters that begin and end שׁלום, as explained above. To these is added the letter ח, which stands for חיות, *vitality,* or חיים, *life.* And in fact the phrase לב שׂמח, meaning *a joyful heart,* has the same numerical value as the word שׁלום, plus 4 for its four letters. (Adding the number of the letters, as in this case, where 4 is added to שׁלום, indicates, according to the Kabbalah, that the word to which the number is added is the cause of the other concept. In this case, peace is the cause of joy.)

The phrase לב שׂמח, *a joyful heart,* has the numerical value 380. When we add 5 for its five letters, the result is 385. This is the numerical value of the word שׁכינה (*Shechinah*), the light of the Divine Presence. Joy causes the light of the Divine Presence to rest upon us. As the Sages say, *"The Divine Presence reveals Itself only where there is joy."*

The numerical value of לו is 36. This represents 6 x 6, or the perfection of *Yesod,* the *sefirah*-attribute represented by the number 6. *Yesod* means *Foundation.* The Talmud (*Sukkah* 45b) states that there are always at least thirty-six righteous ones in the world to receive the Divine Presence. These thirty-six are the *Foundation* of the world's existence.

The final letter of שלום, *peace,* is ם, which is the form taken by the letter מ when it appears at the end of a word. In *gematria,* although ם can be reckoned as 40 (like מ), it is sometimes reckoned as 600. (The final letters, ך-ם-ן-ף-ץ, are assigned the values 500-900.) Taking ם as 600, the numerical value of שלום is 936, which equals 36 × 26. The number 36, as we have seen, represents the perfection of the *sefirah*-attribute of *Yesod (Foundation)*, while 26 is the numerical value of G-d's name. Thus שלום, the peace of the world, depends on the complete purification represented by the number 36, imbued with awareness of G-d's existence and His rulership of this world.

As we have seen, the divine light that fills the soul and body in a state of pure joy is the foundation of man's perfection and health. This is revealed in many ways by a deep understanding of the words *peace* and *joy,* שלום and שמחה.

chapter ten

THE PATRIARCH YAAKOV, SYMBOL OF HEALTH

I n Kabbalah, the *sefirah*-attribute תפארת corresponds to the Patriarch Yaakov (Jacob). *Tiferet* is the third, centrally placed *sefirah*-attribute which follows and harmonizes the *sefirah*-attributes of חסד (*Chesed,* Kindness) and גבורה (*Gevurah*; Strictness, Severity, Judgment). And such was the way of Yaakov, the third of the Patriarchs who was also called Yisrael. It was he who harmonized the qualities of his predecessors Avraham (Abraham), the epitome of Kindness to the right, and Yitzchak (Isaac), who embodied Judgment, to the left.

Yitzchak	Avraham
Gevurah	*Chesed*

Yaakov

Tiferet

Thus the Kabbalah associates Yaakov with the heart, located in the center of the body, while Avraham and Yitzchak are associated with the two arms, one to the right of the heart and the other to the left.

The name יעקב (Yaakov) can be analyzed as the term ע יבק: the letter ע plus the word יבק (**Yabok**), the name of the river that Yaakov crossed just before his struggle with the Angel (**Genesis** 32:23). According to the Kabbalah, **Yabok** alludes to three names of G-d as well as a G-dly attribute associated with Yaakov (see below). The letter ע (with the numerical value of seventy) represents the concept of expansion, for it alludes to the seventy souls of the House of Yaakov – Yaakov's children and grandchildren – who travelled with the Patriarch to Egypt. The term ע יבק, then, can be interpreted as the expansion of the G-dly attribute represented by the term **Yabok** – an expansion first in Yaakov himself and later into the seventy souls of his progeny.

To understand the nature of this G-dly attribute termed **Yabok,** we first must turn to the following list of correspondences:

יבק: *10 + 2 + 100*   *= 112*

Sum of the numerical values of . . . names of G-d :

א-ה-י-ה: *1 + 5 + 10 + 5*   *= 21*

י-ה-ו-ה: *10 + 5 + 6 + 5*   *= 26*

אדנ-י: *1 + 4 + 50 + 10*   *= 65*
                                     112

יבק

א-ה-י-ה	*Keter* (כתר)	brain (מוח)
י-ה-ו-ה	*Tiferet*(תפארת)	heart (לב)
אדנ-י	*Malchut* (מלכות)	liver (כבד)

The numerical value of יבק is 112. Interestingly, this is the sum of the numerical values of the above three unpronounced names of G-d as well as of the Hebrew names of these three bodily organs.

The letter א, like Yaakov, also represents the inner, balancing element that brings harmony among opposite forces (see above, p. 60). The name of this letter, when written out, has the numerical value 111. Ading one for the *kollel* (see Introduction) gives 112.

אלף: $1 + 30 + 80 = 111 + 1 = 112$

The Kabbalah notes that the graphic form of the א has three parts, a central ו with a י above and below. These three parts correspond to the three *sefirah*-attributes, *Chochmah* (*Wisdom*), *Binah* (*Understanding*)

Sum of the numerical values of . . . organs:

מוח:	$40 + 6 + 8$	$= 54$
לב:	$30 + 2$	$= 32$
כבד:	$20 + 2 + 4$	$= \underline{26}$
		112

and **Daat** (**Knowledge**). Taking the final letters of מח,
לב, כבד (**brain, heart, liver**) gives חבד, the Hebrew
initials of חכמה, בינה, דעת, **Chochmah, Binah** and **Daat**.
These three **sefirah**-attributes have their seats, respectively, in the brain, heart, and liver.

To understand the significance of the three Divine
names charted above, we first must look at the **Tree of Life**:

Keter

Binah		Chochmah
	(Daat)	
Gevurah		Chesed
	Tiferet	
Hod		Netzach
	Yesod	

Malchut

At center are **Keter** (Crown), the Divine will, the
first of the G-dly emanations; **Tiferet** (Splendor), the
mediator between Gevurah (Strictness) and Chesed

---

*Tree of Life: The **sefirah**-attributes are often graphically presented
in this format termed the **Tree of Life**, with the **sefirah**-attributes
on the side of Kindness positioned to the right, the **sefirah**-attri-
butes on the side of Severity to the left, and the mediating **sefirah**-
attributes at center.*

(Kindness); and *Malchut* (Kingship). They correspond to the three names of G-d alluded to by the word *Yabok*: Thus the term *Yabok* – hidden in the name Yaakov – represents the balancing and harmonizing forces in the Tree of Life. This is another reason why Yaakov is especially associated with health.

What is more, the numerical value of the name יעקב is 182, while that of תפארת (*Tiferet*) is 281 – the same numerals reversed. Since the numerals of a word's numerical value indicate its *sefirah*-attribute, we can see clearly that יעקב (Yaakov) and תפארת (*Tiferet*) derive from the same spiritual source.

Yaakov, in particular, is associated with health. The Talmud relates: *"Our father Yaakov did not die,"* upon which *Rashi* expounds: *"Rather, he lives forever."*

Visiting the sick, to care for their physical needs, give them encouragement, and pray for them, is an important *mitzvah*. The Talmud (*Nedarim* 39b) states that one who visits a sick person takes away one-sixtieth of his suffering. A hint of this may be found in the story of Joseph's visit to Yaakov. Joseph was told: *"Behold, your father is ill"* (הנה אביך חלה; *Genesis* 48:1). The numerical value of "Behold" (הנה) is 60. When Joseph arrived, *"Yisrael [Yaakov] strengthened himself and sat upon the bed"* (ויתחזק ישראל וישב על המטה; ibid., v. 2). The

---

*Our father Yaakov did not die: **Taanit** 5b.*

final word of this verse is "bed" (המטה), whose numerical value is 59. Thus we see that Yaakov's illness was reduced from 60 to 59, or one-sixtieth.

The Torah relates the story of Yaakov who, while struggling with the Angel, was injured in his thigh. To this the Torah adds that that morning, *"The sun shone for him."* **Rashi** comments: *"It shone for him, [meaning] for his need – that is, to heal his lameness. For it is written: 'The sun of righteousness, and healing in its rays.'"* These verses show Yaakov's special connection with healing as well as the healing power of the sun. Moreover, the Midrash itself compares Yaakov to the sun *(Midrash Rabbah, Parashat Vayetze; see our work, Above the Zodiac).*

The Midrash associates Yaakov with the metal copper (נחשת). This is hinted to in **Genesis,** where Lavan tells Yaakov: *"I have performed divination (נחשתי) [and perceived that] G-d has blessed me because of you."* As is known, copper is associated with healing. When the Children of Israel were bitten by poisonous snakes, G-d

---

It shone for him: ויזרח לו השמש *(Bereshit 32:32).*

Rashi *comments:* ויזרח לו לצרכו לרפאות את צלעתו.

The sun of righteousness: שמש צדקה ומרפא בכנפיה *(Malachi 3:20).*

Lavan tells Yaakov: נחשתי ויברכני ה' בגללך *(30:27).*

*A copper snake: See **Numbers** 21:8. G-d commanded Moses to create an image of a snake (which He called שרף, **Saraf**) and to*

healed them by means of *"a copper snake."* In fact, the words **snake** (נחש) and **copper** share the same three-letter root: נחש.

The Midrash lists those metals corresponding to the four elements (see **Shem Mishmuel** to **Parashat Terumah**):

Iron (ברזל)	Earth (עפר)
Copper (נחשת)	Air (אויר)
Gold (זהב)	Fire (אש)
Silver (כסף)	Water (מים)

Yaakov's metal, copper, corresponds to air. The ancient Kabbalistic work **Sefer Yetzirah (Book of For-**

---

erect it upon a pole for those Jews who had been snake-bitten in the desert to gaze upon and be miraculously cured. **Rashi** explains that Moses had the snake created from copper, since the Hebrew word for copper (נחשת, **nachoshet**) is similar to נחש (**nachash**), the Hebrew word for snake. For nearly 700 years this molten image was preserved in Yerushaliyim by the Jewish nation which, enticed by the idolatrous practices of its neighbors, later began to offer incense to it. King Chizkeya of the Kingdom of Yehuda eventually destroyed the copper relic, which he called **Nechushtan** (נחושתן).

Interestingly, this image as perverted by the Greek-Roman mythology is now recognizable as the symbol of the medical establishment worldwide. Known as the staff of Aesculapius, the Greek-Roman god of medicine, it comprises a lone snake coiled around a

mation) states that the air (אויר) was created with the letter א. As we have just learned, the א is the essential, G-dly letter of both פאר and תפארת (*Tiferet*). The element air is closely linked to health. On the physical level, all healing systems agree that good air and light are essential to health and healing. The Aramaic word אתפח means *to breathe* as well as *to recover from illness*.

The Hebrew word for air is אויר – the same letters as אור (*light*) plus a י. The letter י symbolizes oxygen. As stated in the *Zohar*, G-d first created light and then gave light the letter י to thereby create air.

Substituting the labial letter ב for the labial letter ו

---

knotty wooden pole. It was adopted in 1910 by the American Medical Association as its corporate symbol and later as the insignia of other world medical bodies including the French and British army medical corps, the United States Air Force medical service, and the World Health Organization. Another similar emblem called the **caduceus** (meaning **herald's wand** or **staff**) is also recognizable today as the symbol of formalized medical practice. It consists of **two** snakes coiled around a winged pole and is commonly seen on medical-product packaging around the globe.

The Hebrew word for **air** is אויר (**avir**): Note the similarity to the English **air**.

The letter י symbolizes oxygen: This is seen clearly in the Hebrew word מים (**mayim, water**), whose two מ's parallel water's two hydrogen molecules while its י represents the sole oxygen molecule of H_2O.

As stated in the **Zohar**: Beginning of **Bereshit**.

G-d first created light: On Day One of the Six Days of Creation,

of the word אויר produces the letters בריא (*healthy*). Thus Yaakov is associated with the metal copper and the element air, both of which are especially connected to health.

The Hebrew vowel *cholam* (חולם), whose root is חלם, is associated by the Kabbalah with the Patriarch Yaakov. This is also the root of the word החלמה, which means *recuperation* or *convalescence*. Rearranging its letters produces the root לחם, whose principle meaning is *to join together*. Thus להלחים means *to weld*. And so is bread known as לחם, for it is the staff of life, the food that can fuse together one's soul and body, thereby giving life and health.

Similarly, these same three letters in different order form the roots of other words related to the concept of joining. A dream (חלום) – Yaakov's dreams are well-documented in Torah – joins together the upper and

---

G-d said—יהי אור—"Let there be light." Physical air was created on the Second Day.

Substituting the ב with . . . ו: The labial letters are ב,ו,מ,פ.

(For a more detailed discussion of the relationship between air and health, as reflected in the Hebrew language, see the first three chapters of our work, **From Hinduism Back To Judaism**.)

The Hebrew vowel **cholam**: The **cholam** corresponds to the long o common to English and can be indicated in two ways: full or incomplete. Its full indication comprises the Hebrew letter ו and a sole superscript dot. Incomplete, it is indicated simply by its superscript dot.

The numerical value of לחם:

lower worlds. **Salt** (מלח) prevents foods from decomposition by welding together their component parts. And **forgiveness** (מחילה) is the G-dly act that brings old friends back together again.

The numerical value of לחם is 78 – three times 26, the numerical value of the Ineffable Name (י-ה-ו-ה). This is one of the reasons why, when beginning a meal, we first dip the bread three times in salt before eating.

The letters of the word לחם are the initials of the words לב (*heart*), מוח (*brain*) and חיים (*life*), because bread gives life to both the brain and heart.

Each of the three Patriarchs of the Jewish people – Avraham, Yitzchak, and Yaakov – is called a "chariot" of The Name, a reference to their selfless devotion to G-d's will. Since Yaakov is the third of the three Patriarchs, he combines and completes the attributes of his predecessors. Therefore, Yaakov can be said to correspond to three times the numerical value of The Name – 78, the numerical value of חלם – a reference to the Hebrew vowel corresponding to Yaakov.

The Kabbalah assigns colors to all the *sefirah-*

לחם: *30 + 8 + 40*   *= 78*

י-ה-ו-ה: *10 + 5 + 6 + 5 = 26 × 3 = 78*

"Chariot" of The Name: In Hebrew, מרכבה (mercava). Just as a chariot is motivated solely by the will of its driver, so too the Patriarchs, who nullified their will solely to that of their Creator.

attributes. The colors assigned to חסד (Kindness), גבורה (Strict Judgment), and תפארת (Splendor) are:

Gevurah:
Red

Chesed:
White

Tiferet:
Green

The apple, a symbol of healing, is associated with these three colors. Apples are red on the outside, white on the inside, and their leaves are green. Yaakov, too, is associated with apples. Just before blessing him, his father Yitzchak declared: *"See, the fragrance of my son is like the fragrance of a field which G-d has blessed."* On this **Rashi** quotes the Sages: *"This is the field of apples."* Moreover, in the **Song of Songs** King Solomon writes: *"Revigorate me with apples."*

Aramaic, the language of the Talmud, the Zohar, and other writings, derives from Hebrew, the Holy Tongue. As mentioned above, the Aramaic אתפח means *to*

The Kabbalah assigns colors: See **Kehilat Yaakov,** s.v. ירוק.

The apple [is] a symbol of healing: As is reflected in the folk saying, "An apple a day keeps the doctor away!"

See, the fragrance ...: ראה ריח בני כריח שדה אשר ברכו ה' (Genesis 27:27).

Rashi: וזהו שדה תפוחים כך דרשו רז"ל.

Revigorate me with apples: רפדוני בתפוחים (2:5).

breathe and *to recover from illness*. Most interestingly, its root letters תפח are those of the the word תפוח – Hebrew for *apple*.

Tiferet, the quality corresponding to Yaakov, is assigned the color green – the color of healing. Green in Hebrew is ירק. Looking at the Hebrew alphabet, we find:

א ב ג ד ה ו ז ח ט **י כ** ל מ נ ס ע פ צ **ק ר ש** ת

כ	follows	י
ש	follows	ר
ר	follows	ק

What follows ירק in the Hebrew alphabet is the word כשר (*kasher*), meaning *fit, valid, sound*. Exchanging the palatal כ with the palatal ק makes קשר (*kesher,* connection). When one achieves Yaakov's attribute of *Tiferet,* each of the 248 organs of the body connects (קשר) with its spiritual source, resulting in fitness and soundness (כשר).

[Green is] the color of healing: Green is the traditional color of hospital operating rooms as well as surgical clothing.

Yaakov: The third Patriarch, he is associated with the unifying faculty of דעת (Daat, Knowledge), the third of the three intellectual soul-powers. Daat is the conclusive intellect-power that not only unites its precursors, the creative Chochmah (Wisdom) and the developmental Binah (Understanding), but also unites intellect with emotion to bring one's learning into action.

The word כשר (*kasher*) also refers to food that meets the Torah's standards of permissibility. This hints at the importance of food that is *kasher* in building a soul and body that are fit, in which all the component parts have the right connection (קשר) with each other.

The numerical value of ירק – written in its "short" or deficient form without the vowel ו – is equal to that of יש, which means *existence*. One of the four Hebrew words for man, איש (meaning a refined man, such as a righteous person or leader) can be analyzed as the letters יש plus א. Since, as mentioned above (p. 60), the letter א is a reference to both G-d and Torah, the word איש tells much: that G-d (א) is the source of man's existence, and by acquiring the Torah wisdom (א) that is G-d's will, man maintains his existence. By doing so, physical man becomes a refined man (איש) and thus shows that G-d and G-dliness (א) exist (יש).

The other color used by doctors, nurses and hospitals is white. In Kabbalah this color, besides being associated (as we saw above) with the *sefirah*-attribute of

---

*יש: Note the similarity to the English **is**.*

The numerical value of ירק:

> *ירק: 10 + 200 + 100   = 310*

[The numerical value of] יש:

> *יש :   10 + 300   = 310*

*Four Hebrew words for **man**: אנוש, אדם, איש, גבר.*

Chessed (*Kindness*) is also associated with the highest world, *Keter* (*Crown*) and with the *sefirah*-attribute just below it, *Chochmah* (*Wisdom*). *Keter* is the primary source of emanation of all existence (see below, p. 116 sec. 18) and hence the ultimate source of health.

White in Hebrew is לבן (*lavan*). The corresponding English letters are: *l. b. n.* These letters are the basis of the English word *balance,* which indicates the basic quality needed for health. They are also the basis of the word *noble* [*lavan* pronounced in reverse is *noble*], which is appropriate to the high position of the *sefirah*-attribute of *Keter.* [The Kabbalah says that *Keter,* the *Crown,* belongs to the world of *Atzilus* (*Nobility*)."

chapter eleven

SHABBAT AND YAAKOV

S habbat, the Sabbath Day of Rest, is the time
that heals.

The Talmud states that when visiting the ill on
Shabbat one should say: *"It is a day of rest from crying
out, but recovery is near to come."* On Shabbat, says the
Ben Yehoyada, there is no need to request healing, for
Shabbat is a day of kindness when healing comes of its
own accord.

Commenting on the verse *"Please, G-d, heal her,
please,"* the **Arizal** alludes to the kabbalistic understanding of healing, namely, that healing *"sweetens the five
severities (**Gevurot**)."* That is, healing joins the quality of
Chesed (Kindness) to that of **Gevurah (Strict Judgment)** resulting in the quality of **Tiferet (Splendor)**,

---

The Talmud **(Shabbat** 12a): שבת היא מלזעוק ורפואה קרובה לבא
*[On Shabbat] there is no need to request healing: On weekdays
one says:* רפואה שלמה—*"[May you have] a complete recovery!"*
Please, G-d , heal her, please: א-ל נא רפא נא לה *(**Numbers**
12:13).*

which is the harmonious balance of **Chesed** and **Gevurah** by raising the latter to its source in **Chesed**.

This is evident in the numerical value of a Hebrew word meaning **healing**: רפוא. Its numerical value is 287. With the addition (= 1) of the **kollel** (see Introduction) we have 288, which is the combined numerical value of חסד and גבורה. When the **Chesed** (**Kindness**) of Shabbat is joined to the **Gevurah** (**Strict Judgment**) of sickness, the result is healing (רפוא) through the quality of **Tiferet**.

Healing "sweetens the five severities": המתקת הדינים

[The numerical value of] רפוא:

200 + 80 + 6 + 1 = 287 + 1 = 288

Addition of the **kollel** [כולל]: As is known, Hebrew words are based upon conceptual roots, most of which comprise three letters. These roots — for example, חשב meaning **think**, דבר meaning **speak**, עשה meaning **do** — have not developed etymologically as have those of other tongues but are Divine in origin. Furthermore, the combination of each root's component letters in such specific order — that is, the concept of thinking as represented by first ח followed by ש and then ב, for example — not only communicates the meaning of that root but actually describes the G-d ly life-force as revealed through the root's letters. For it is through the twenty-two letters of the Holy Tongue that G-d continually creates and sustains Creation. That is, a thing exists — whether it be material or spiritual, physical or conceptual — solely because of the G-d ly life-force channelled through each particular root-letter of that thing's Hebrew name.

Hebrew letters, therefore, are conduits of this G-d ly life-force. Their written forms, states R. Schneur Zalman of Liadi in his **Shaar HaYichud VeHaEmunah (Gate of Unity and Faith)**, "indicate the pattern of the flow and the manifestation of the light and the life-force and the power which is revealed and flows through [them]."

As mentioned above (p. 50, sec. 6), the root letters רפא (*to heal*) can be rearranged to spell פאר, the quality the *Arizal* states is the spiritual source of healing. As

---

As such, the Hebrew roots composed of these G-d ly letter-conduits are by themselves not of this physical world but apart from it, above it, transcendent. It is only when a root is conjugated (by the addition of other Hebrew letters and vowels) that its conceptual meaning is drawn down into the physical realm and made to describe the plurality of physical creation.

For instance, the addition of the prefix מ, the suffix ה, and various vowels so conjugates — that is, draws down — the Hebrew root-concept חשב into the nominal form מחשבה and thereby vivifies and communicates the very earthly intellectual process called thought.

Once conjugated, a Hebrew root not only retains an intrinsic connection to the spiritual source of each of its component letters but also reflects a general, all-comprehensive influence that transcends the sum of its parts. This all-comprehensive, general power is represented by the **kollel** which is, quite logically, equal to 1, the number representing both unity and sheer simplicity. Moreover, when added to the numerical value of a word, the **kollel** describes the Hebrew word's ever-present attachment to and dependence on its spiritual source Above.

A clarifying example: the Hebrew word for **covenant** —ברית (**brit**) —has a numerical value of 612.

ברית: 2 + 200 + 10 + 400 = 612.

By adding the all-encompassing **kollel** (= 1) we can see more clearly the relationship between the concept of convenant and the 613 Scriptural commandments as given to the Jewish people.

A related method of numerical Torah interpretation adds the number of letters of a word to that word's numerical value.

[The] combined numerical value of חסד and גבורה:

חסד:	8 + 60 + 4	= 72
גבורה:	3 + 2 + 6 + 200 + 5	= 216
		288

---

mentioned above, the numerical value of פאר according to the **Al-Bam** transformation is forty-five. Moreover, the ordinal numerical value of שבת equals forty-five as well − another hint of the healing power of Shabbat.

Moreover, when we write out the names of the letters of פאר, the total numerical value is 702, which equals the numerical value of the word שבת (**Shabbat**). The letters of פאר can be spelled:

פא (*pe*)	81
אלף (*alef*)	111
ריש (*resh*)	510
	702

שבת (**Shabbat**): 300 + 2 + 400 = 702

These are hints of the healing power of Shabbat.

That the Shabbat is a day of healing is seen in one of the four names derived from the Tetragrammaton (י-ה-ו-ה). The name מה also yields the numerical value of forty-five. This name refers to the **sefirah**-attribute **Tiferet,** and as we have seen, **Tiferet** (תפארת) derives from the root פאר − the spiritual source of healing.

Ordinal numerical value of שבת: 21 + 2 + 22 = 45.

Through this method of Torah interpretation, a Hebrew word is calculated according to each letter's position in the Hebrew alphabet. Here, the letter ש is the twenty-first letter of the alphabet; the ב is the second, and ת, the twenty-second. Thus שבת totals to 45.

The number 45 is also the numerical value of אדם, *man*. The nation of Israel are also referred to as אדם. This shows that man (אדם) reaches his perfection through *Tiferet*.

Sickness, says the author of *Ben Ish Chai,* involves a distortion of the letter י, the suspended point representing the *sefirah*-attribute *Chochmah* (*Wisdom*). This is seen in the verse *"G-d will sustain him on his sickbed."* Each of the two words composing the Hebrew term *sickbed* – ערש דוי – permutes the letter י. How so? The word ערש contains the disordered letters of עשר, meaning *ten,* the numerical value of the letter י. And similarly, the word דוי contains the same letters as the name of the letter יוד(י). The implication is: when the י is in its proper, undistorted order, it is particularly connected with health; distorted, it leads to debilitating sickness, רחמנא לצלן.

Interestingly, states the *Ben Ish Chai,* it is the letter י that prevails on Shabbat. For this letter not only represents *Chochmah* but also the *sefirah*-attribute *Daat* (דעת, Knowledge). This is seen in the *milui* of the name of the letter י; the sum of their numerical values equals 476, the numerical value of the word בדעת, meaning *with knowledge.* The *milui* of the word שבת is also 476.

From this we learn that י, the letter of healing, not only prevails on the Shabbat but is the spiritual essence of the day of healing, as it is written: *"To know* (לדעת) *that I am G-d Who sanctifies you"* (לדעת כי אני ד' מקדשכם; *Exodus* 31:13). *Daat (Knowledge)*, like *Tiferet (Splendor)*, is a *sefirah*-attribute that harmonizes opposite forces (see above, p. 78).

One of the names of G-d is י-ה. Its numerical value is 15. When we add the word רפאות (*healing*), the resulting phrase, רפאות י-ה can be translated: "the healing of God."

Milui:

The letter י itself can be spelled thus: יוד.

י	spelled יוד: 10 + 6 + 4	= 20
ו	spelled ויו: 6 + 10 + 6	= 22
ד	spelled דלת: 4 + 30 + 400	= 434
		476

בדעת: 2 + 4 + 70 + 400 = 476

Milui of the word שבת:

ש is written שין. The inner letters are ין: 10 + 50 = 60

ב is written בית. The inner letters are ית: 10 + 400 = 410

ת is written תו. The inner letter is ו: 6 = 6

476

— 97 —

Its numerical value is 702. This is also the the numerical value of שבת (*Shabbat*). The two letters of this name, י and ה, represent respectively the *sefirah*-attributes **Chochmah (*Wisdom*)** and **Binah (*Understanding*)**. **Daat** is the intermediary *sefirah*-attribute that harmonizes these two **attributes,** just as **Tiferet (*Splendor*)** harmonizes the attributes **Chessed (*Kindness*)** and **Gevurah (*Strict Judgment*)**. Thus we see that the spiritual essence of Shabbat is the same spiritual quality that is the essence of healing.

The word שבת can be interpreted as ש plus בת. The letter ש represents fire, for fire, states the **Sefer Yetzirah,** is created by means of the letter ש. The ש also represents radiant light, for in fact this letter comprises the letters זיו, the Hebrew word for *ray* or *radiant light.* More tellingly, the letter ש represents the spiritual light of the **Shechinah** (שכינה), the Divine Presence on earth. And the letters בת spell the Hebrew word for *daughter* – a reference to both the Jewish woman, the *"daughter of Yisrael,"* whose weekly kindling of the Shabbat can-

---

רפאות י-ה: 200 + 80 + 1 + 6 + 400 + 10 + 5   = 702

שבת :   = 702

*The letter ש represents fire: **Sefer Yetzirah** 3:3. This connection is seen in the letter's very shape — flames rising to their supernal source.*

Jewish woman's kindling: The kindling of Shabbat candles has for millenia given testimony to the other-worldliness of the Day of Rest.

dles elicits the Divine Presence on earth, and to the נשמה, the Jewish soul. Shabbat, then, is the day of radiant light (זיו) – the day in which G-d's Presence is drawn down to the physical realm by means of the Jewish woman's kindling of Shabbat candles. This is a source of joy and health for the Jewish soul – the souls of the daughter of Yisrael and her family.

Our forefather Yaakov is especially connected with Shabbat. The Torah states that upon Yaakov's arrival in Shechem, *"he camped facing the city."* The Midrash explains this to mean that Yaakov immediately established the Shabbat boundary of his camp. Therefore does the Prophet declare: *"If you refrain from pursuing your needs on Shabbat, on My holy day, and if you make Shabbat a day of pleasure ... I shall feed you the inheritance of your father Yaakov."*

The glistening of Shabbat candles, states the **Shulchan Aruch,** the Code of Jewish Law, brings peace to the home and is therefore termed עונג שבת *(oneg Shabbat)* — Sabbath joy. Specifically, the **mitzvah** is to eat the Shabbat evening meal by this light. Commanded to both men and women, the commandment to kindle Shabbat candles is especially dear to Jewish women, for hers is the realm of the home and its needs. For more insights see our work, **The Mystical Glory of Shabbath and Festivals.**

He camped facing the city: ויחן את פני העיר *(Genesis 33:18).*

Midrash explains . . . the Shabbat boundary: **(Bereshit Rabba** 79:6).

Shabbat boundary: The Torah stipulates that a Jew must not overstep a boundary of 2,000 **amah** (approximately 3,600 feet) from his

As mentioned above, the metal associated with both Yaakov and healing is copper (נחשת). The numerical equivalent of נחשת is also that of יום שבת, the "Sabbath Day."

Since the observance of Shabbat is considered equal to the observance of all other commandments together, we can therefore deduce the spiritual wholeness – and spiritual health – that is brought by observance of the Day of Rest.

*place of residence on the Holy Day Shabbat. Though not yet given to the nation at the time of his coming to Shechem, the Patriarch Yaakov, as did his fathers Avraham and Yitzchak, upheld all **mitzvot** of the Torah, including this **mitzvah** of the Shabbat boundary.*

If you refrain ... Yaakov: אם תשיב משבת רגלך עשות חפצך ביום קדשי וקראת לשבת ענג והאכלתיך נחלת יעקב אביך (*Isaiah 58:13-14*).

Numerical equivalent[s] of יום שבת ... נחשת:

נחשת: *50 + 8 + 300 + 400*   = 758

יום שבת: *10 + 6 + 40 + 300 + 2 + 400*   = 758

Shabbat is . . . the equivalent of all other commandments: (**Chulin** *5a;* **Rambam, Hilchot Shabbat** *30:15*).

chapter twelve

RESTORING THE LOST SPARKS

We saw above that the numerical value of *healing* (רפוא) is 287. The number 287 is also the combined numerical value of *good* (טוב, 17) and *bad* (רע, 270). This shows that healing makes constructive use of man's good and evil inclinations, combining them together, but with the good in the dominant position (see below, p. 184).

The same letters that spell רפוא also spell רופא, meaning *he heals*. Hence רופא also has the numerical value 288 (with the addition of one for the *kollel*). This is the word used in the *Shemoneh-Esreh* Prayer in the blessing for healing, which concludes: "... *Who heals the sick of His people Israel*" (רופא חולי עמו ישראל). The *Arizal* points out that the initials of this phrase — רחע"י — also add up to 288. He states that when reciting this blessing one should think of the 288 sparks of G-dliness lost in Israel's exile, sparks which we must rectify and restore to their proper place.

The number 288 is also the numerical value of פרח (*parach*), meaning to flower, indicating that through the struggle between good and evil, and the struggle to balance Kindness and Strict Judgment, a person "flowers" to his full perfection.

One of the main ways through which we rectify these sparks is by reciting the proper blessings over the food we eat. The fallen sparks are concealed in the food, and we elevate them by incorporating them into our body with the blessing.

Thus the word for "food" is אכל, which can be analyzed as כל א. The first part of the word (א) represents the Divine. The second part (כל) means *everything*. Thus the Hebrew word for food indicates that sparks of the Divine are found in everything, and are rectified particularly in the food we eat.

In Kabbalah, כל indicates the *sefirah*-attribute called **Yesod (Foundation)**. This *sefirah*-attribute acts as the final transition point leading to **Malchut (Kingship)**, where G-d's kingship is fully revealed and acknowledged. Thus the structure of the word אכל – א כל – shows us that the way we eat our food is an important means for bringing about the Messianic Age, the time of complete revelation of G-d's kingship. Through אכל, *food,* the Divine (א) is brought to the level of **Yesod** (כל), making it ready to be revealed in our world. (See above, p. 67, the discussion of the importance of the letter א in the words אדם, ארץ, and אמת.)

Man was created in the *"image of God"* (צלם אלקים; **Genesis** 1:27). But when man sinned and went into exile (first from the Garden of Eden and later from the

Land of Israel) the *"image of God"* (*tzelem Elokim*) in him became defective; parts of it − i.e., divine "sparks" − were lost in exile. The terms "spark" (ניצוץ) and *"image of God"* (צלם אלקים) have the same numerical value: 246.

ניצוץ: 50 + 10 + 90 + 6 + 90   = 246

צלם אלקים: 90+30+40 + 1+30+5+10+40 = 246

When we add 2 for the two words of the phrase, the numerical value of צלם אלקים comes to 248. The Sages say that 248 is the number of organs in the human body [which was created in the *"image of God."*] This is yet another example of the principle, *"From my flesh I see G-d."*

Every created thing contains its "spark," which is its portion of the *"image of God."* These sparks need to be repaired, raised up, returned to their proper place, retrieved from their exile and captivity. When this is accomplished, then the *"image of God"* in man will be restored to its original perfection and will be **complete,** תמים.

This perfection comes about when the soul (*neshamah*) is in control of the body. The body is the vehicle of the Evil Inclination (***Yetzer Hara***). For example, the urge of the body is to consume food blindly when hunger is felt. The body is not concerned whether a blessing is recited over the food. The soul, if permitted to manifest itself, constrains the body, permitting it to eat only after the blessing is recited. The blessing remedies the lost sparks; and this leads to the perfection of the *"image of God"* in man.

Thus the correct combination of body and soul makes man perfect. When G-d gave Abraham the covenant of circumcision, it enabled Abraham to be in complete spiritual control of his body. At that time G-d told him: *"Walk before Me and be perfect"* (התהלך לפני והיה תמים; **Genesis** 17:1).

Healing is always a matter of balance between opposite forces. (In modern terms, "holistic" medicine strives to treat man as a totality of body and soul.)

This concept is inherent in the Hebrew language, for the numerical value of the word **perfect** (תמים) is equal to the numerical value of the phrase, "body and soul" (גוף ונשמה).

תמים:	$400 + 40 + 10 + 40$	$= 490$
גוף ונשמה:	$3+6+80 + 6+50+300+40+5$	$= 490$

The number 490 can be seen as representing the forty-nine gates of wisdom (see **Rosh Hashanah** 21b) and the forty-nine gates of purity, brought to perfection through all ten levels of Creation: $49 \times 10 = 490$.

According to the Kabbalah, the *"image of God"* (צלם אלקים) is seen in the aura, the spiritual light that surrounds every individual, and upon which his or her life is dependent. This is another reason why the word רפואה (**healing**) contains the words פה (**mouth, opening**) and אור (**light**). Healing makes an opening (פה) for the light (אור) of the aura to enter the body. This is the light of the צלם אלקים, the *"image of G-d"*. (For more concerning the aura, see below, p. 144)

[In light of the above, it is interesting to note the similarity in sound among the English words: "heal," "halo," "whole,"and "holy."]

chapter thirteen

TORAH THE SOURCE OF HEALTH

Yaakov's connection to healing is seen through his association with Torah, as it is written: *"You give truth to Yaakov."* Truth, states the Talmud, is the Torah itself, as is written: *"Truth is Torah."*

More specifically, immediately upon leaving Egypt the Jewish people were informed that the Torah is for them the source of healing: *"If you listen to the voice of G-d your G-d, and do what is right in His eyes, and listen to His commandments, and observe all His decrees – all the diseases that I put upon Egypt, I shall not put upon you; for I, G-d, am your doctor."* (אם שמוע תשמע לקול ה'‏ אלקיך והישר בעיניו תעשה והאזנת למצותיו ושמרת כל חקיו כל המחלה אשר שמתי במצרים לא אשים עליך כי אני ה' רפאך; *Exodus* 15:26).

This verse is explained on a deeper level by The Maggid of Trisk in his work ***Magen Avraham.*** He says that when a Jew speaks words of Torah and prayer with

---

You give truth to Yaakov: תתן אמת ליעקב (*Micha* 7:20).

Truth is Torah: אמת זו תורה (*Berachot* 5b).

his voice it brings about the unification of "voice" (קול) and "speech" (דבור). Each of these terms corresponds to a name of G-d. "Voice" (קול) corresponds to the name י-ה-ו-ה, which refers to the unknowable inner essence of G-d, while "speech" corresponds to the name אדנ-י (*Adnut*), which refers to G-d manifest in the natural world He has created. The unification of voice and speech in our lower world brings about, in the upper world, unification of the letters of G-d's Name, and that causes both spiritual and physical healing for all Israel.

[It should be noted that the total numerical value of the words קול and דבור (*voice* and *speech*) is 348, which is the numerical value of שמח, *happy*. This shows that the unification referred to here brings joy to the world. As we have seen (above, p. 42) joy is a basic cause of health.

The letter ש, the first letter of שמח, represents fire, which rises upwards. Thus it stands for the heavenly realm, and corresponds to קול (*voice*), which is the heavenly aspect of communication. The letter מ, the second letter of שמח, represents water, which flows downwards. Thus it stands for the earthly realm, and corresponds to דבור (*speech*) the earthly aspect of communication.

We saw above (p. 124) that שמח (*happy*), like שלום (*peace*), is a word that represents the harmonizing of opposites. We also saw (p. 40) that the name of G-d, י-ה, represents the harmonizing of opposites because it com-

bines both **Chochmah** and **Binah**. Thus when we take
the numerical value of שמח, 348, and add the digits
together (3 + 4 + 8), the result is 15, the numerical value of י-ה.]

Magen Avraham writes:

> This is the meaning of the verse, "If you
> listen to the voice of G-d your G-d."
> The voice alludes to the name י-ה-ו-ה,
> Blessed is He. That is why it says: ". . .
> to the voice of G-d your G--d." The
> next phrase, "...and do (תעשה) what is
> right in His eyes," refers to the world of
> Action (עשיה). This world [the lowest,
> most physical of the four worlds] corre-
> sponds to the aspect of the soul called
> **nefesh** [the lowest, most physical of the
> five parts of the soul]. The **nefesh** cor-
> responds to the final ה in the name
> י-ה-ו-ה, and to the term "speech" (דבור).
> This refers to our speaking words of
> Torah and prayer with our voices and
> our speech, through which we cause the
> unification of the names י-ה-ו-ה and
> אדנ-י (Adnut). This destroys and re-
> moves from us every portion of evil and
> contamination and draws down upon
> us His Divine Presence, Blessed is He.
> Through this lower unification one
> causes the upper unification of the two
> letters י-ה of G-d's Name.

This is the meaning of the next phrase in our verse: *"... and listen to His commandments."* The word "listen" (הַאֲזַנְתָּ) comes from the same linguistic root as "ear" (אֹזֶן). The *Arizal* points out that it has the same numerical value as the Name of G-d when the names of the letters are written out in full and one is added for the *kollel*.

י	יוד	20
ה	הי	15
ו	ואו	13
ה	הי	15
		63

Plus one for the *kollel*: = 64

אֹזֶן: 1 + 6 + 7 + 50   = 64

[The root of אֹזֶן is אזן, which is also the root of אִיזוּן, *balance*. Listening (הַאֲזַנְתָּ) to G-d's commandments brings a person to a state of balance (אִיזוּן).]

According to the Kabbalah, this particular way of writing G-d's Name in full, which has the numerical value 63, corresponds to the first ה in G-d's Name. [There are four ways of writing out the Name in full, as shown above, (see p. 124). Each of these four ways corresponds to one of the four letters of the Name.] Through the unification of the names י-ה-ו-ה and אדנ-י, on the level of the letters ו-ה, through this (as is known from the holy *Zohar*) the letter ו reaches down to the lower ה [that is, the second ה of the name] to raise it up to the upper ה [that is, the first ה of the name], which corresponds to the higher form of repentance (*teshuvah*). [Thus far we find the last three letters of the Name unified.]

The next phrase in our verse is: "... *and observe all His decrees.*" The word **decree** (**chukah**) refers to a commandment whose reason is beyond the grasp of the human intellect [for example, the prohibition against wearing a combination of wool and linen]. It alludes to the *sefirah*-attribute called Wisdom (**Chochmah**), which is represented by the י in G-d's Name. For **Chochmah** is above our grasp, and thus is like the decrees of the Torah, which seem to have no logical explanation. We know that they are on a very high level, but it is not within our power to taste the taste of the sweet light that is in it.

Thus, through the unification of voice with speech one causes the unification of all four letters of G-d's Name, Blessed is He. The result is: "*All the diseases that I put upon Egypt, I shall not put upon you; for I, G-d, am your doctor.*" That is, when there is unification in the name י-ה-ו-ה, healing is drawn down upon all the sick of Israel, healing of body and soul. This is hinted at by the phrase, "*For I, G-d, am your doctor*" (כי אני ה רפאך).

The quality of truth, which is especially associated with Yaakov, is the source of health and long life. The classic work of Torah ethics, **Orchot Tzaddikim (Shaar Ha'emet)** states: "*Someone who speaks only truth will live* *and achieve long life."* The Talmud tells of a city called Kushta. As long as a person remained in the city he would not die. The name Kushta is Aramaic for "truth."

Kehillat Yaakov states that the metal corresponding to Torah is copper. And as we have seen above, copper is closely connected with Yaakov and with healing.

For some, the center of life is in the body. The English word to "live" is similar to "love" and "liver," and to Hebrew *lev* (לב), meaning the *heart*. But from a more spiritual viewpoint, the center of life is in the brain. Thus when we write the letters of מוח (*brain*) in reverse order, they spell חום (*warmth*) which is almost identical to חיים (*life*). Moreover, the numerical value of חיים is equal to that of חכם, meaning *wise* or *learned* (see above, p. 40). The true essence of life is wisdom.

This fact has practical consequences in Jewish Law, with regard to unintentional murder. Someone who kills unintentionally must be exiled to one of the cities of refuge (***arei miklat***). ***Rambam*** states: *"If a Torah scholar is sentenced to exile in a city of refuge, his teacher is sent into exile with him, as it is said: `[He shall flee to one of those cities] and live'* (וחי; ***Deuteronomy*** *4:42). [This means:] `Do for him whatever is necessary in order that he should live.' And for the wise and those who seek wisdom, life without Torah-study is like death. Likewise, if a teacher is sentenced to exile, his yeshivah is sent into exile with him"* (***Hilchot Rotzeach*** *9:1*).

"Who is wise? He who foresees events in their infan-

cy" (*Tamid* 32a). Wisdom means proper sight. The wise person sees straight ahead and does not worry. This is true life.

The Talmud asks:

> What is [the meaning of] the verse, "Hear, for I shall speak important matters (**negidim**)"? [It means:] To what may the words of the Torah be compared? To a ruler (**negid**). Just as a ruler has the power to cause death or give life, so the words of the Torah have the power to cause death or give life. This is what Rava said: "For those who deal with it right-handedly it is an elixir of life; for those who deal with it left-handedly, it is an elixir of death."

Indeed, the Talmud states elsewhere:

> R. Yosef bar Chama said that R. Sheshet said: "What is [the meaning of] the verse: "Length of days is on its [the Torah's] right; on its left, wealth and

---

The Talmud asks: (**Shabbat** 88b).

Hear, for I shall speak . . .: שמעו כי נגידים אדבר (**Proverbs** 8:6).

For those who deal with it right-handedly: Who are these? Explains **Rashi**: "Those who engage in it with all their strength, obsessed to know its secret. . . ."

The Talmud states elsewhere: (**Shabbat** 63a).

honor."? [It means:] Those who deal with it right-handedly will be long-lived. . . Those who deal with it left-handedly . . . will not be long-lived."

We conclude: When Torah is on the right side – when the Torah is learned with the right intentions – it is an "elixir of life"; on the left side – when it is learned for insincere or even sinister reasons – it is an "elixir of death."

This is seen in the very letters of the Hebrew root רפא – *to heal.* Recalling that the letter א represents G-dliness, wisdom, and Torah-study, and that the letter ר represents the head (ראש), we can analyze this root as it is permuted into two forms:

פרא   פאר

(wild)   (splendor)

In the positive form פאר, the א is found to the right of the ר, while in the destructive form (פרא, wild) the א is found to the left of the ר. The splendor (פאר) of Torah is revealed when one's Torah study is, figuratively

---

*Those who deal with it right-handedly: Says **Rashi**: "for its own sake."*

*Those who deal with it left-handedly: Says **Rashi**: " ... will not be long-lived."*

Length of days: ארך ימים בימינה בשמאולה עשר וכבוד (Pro-*verbs* 3:16).

— 113 —

speaking, "on the right side." And as we have seen, פאר
is the spiritual source of health.

Shem MiShmuel (to *Genesis* 2:17) finds a similar
pattern in the words מת (*met,* "dead") and תם (*tam,*
"pure") whose common ת represents Torah (תורה).
Through their stark disparity of meaning, these two
words emphasize the significance of letter position in Hebrew roots. The word מת, with its ת on the left, means
"dead"; the word תם, with its ת to the right, means "pure,
whole, complete." And thus is Yaakov characterized by
Scripture: *"A pure* (תם) *man, sitting in tents." ·Rashi*
expounds "tents" to mean "the tent [Torah academy] of
Shem [Noah's son] and the tent of Ever [the great-grand-
son of Shem]."

Torah brings life. When studied with the proper attitude, it is the source of spiritual and emotional, physical and intellectual health.

This theme is further developed in connection with
the verse: *"You shall place these words of Mine upon your
heart..."* Commenting on the word שמתם ("You shall
place"), the Talmud offers an alternative reading based
on the interchange of the sibilant letters ס and שם תם –
ש, "a complete remedy." The Talmud adds: *"The Torah is
comparable to an elixir* (סם) *of life."* Here again, we find

---

A pure man, sitting in tents: איש תם ישב אהלים *(Genesis 25:27).*
You shall place: ושמתם את דברי אלה על לבבכם *(Deuteronomy*
11:18).

in the word חם an allusion to Yaakov and his total devotion and pure motivation in Torah study.

A similar lesson is derived from the verse, *"This is the Torah that Moshe put (שם) in front of the Children of Yisrael."* On this, too the Talmud substitutes סם (*elixer*) for שם (*put*), and comments: *"If he merits, [the Torah] becomes his elixir of life. If he does not merit, [the Torah] becomes his elixir of death."*

סם: **Drug, medicine, elixir.** *The Hebrew word* סם *also means* **poison.**

The sibilant letters ס *and* ש: *The sibilant letters* ר,ץ,ש,ס,ז *are pronounced by expelling air between the teeth, with the tongue held flat. Although grammarians categorize the* ר *as a guttural, the Sages of the Kabbalah classified it as a sibilant. See* **Sefer Yetzirah.**

The Torah is comparable: נמשלה תורה כסם חיים *(Kiddushin 30b).*

This is the Torah: וזאת התורה אשר שם משה לפני בני ישראל *(Deuteronomy 4:44).*

The Talmud...comments: (Yoma 72b).

If he merits: זכה נעשית לו סם חיים לא זכה נעשית לו סם מיתה.

chapter fourteen

THE CROWN

The 613 Scriptural commandments plus the seven Rabbinic commandments are said to compose the "crown" of Torah, for the total of 613 and 7 is 620, the numerical value of the word *crown* (כתר). Interestingly, with the addition of the *kollel* (1), the Hebrew word for health — בריאות — shares this same numerical value. As is taught, the addition of the *kollel* to a word indicates that word's intrinsic connection to and dependence upon the second word to which its numerical value now equals. For the second word is the root or spiritual source of the first. Thus is seen that the *sefirah*-attribute of כתר (*Crown*) is the spiritual source of בריאות, *health.*

בריאות *[plus the* **kollel** *equals]* כתר:

כתר:	20 + 400 + 200	= 620
בריאות:	2 + 200 + 10 + 1 + 6 + 400	= 619
	+ 1	= 620

Keter *is the...first emanation: This is seen in the Ineffable Name of G-d (י-ה-ו-ה). As taught in the* **Zohar***, the four letters of The Name*

Another word for **health** is אֲרוּכָה. The root of this word is אָרַךְ, which is also a term used to refer to **Keter**.

As its name suggests, כתר (**Keter**) is the crowning, encompassing first emanation of emanations of G-dliness called **sefirah**-attribute. As such it cannot be known; it is too sublime, too close in spiritual intensity to the Essence of G-d to be detailed. As the first emanation, **Keter** is the spiritual bridge that connects the Essence of G-d with and unifies all the **sefirah**-attributes. This is reflected in the similarity of the word כתר to the word קשר (**connection**). Indeed, interchanging the palatal letter כ with the palatal ק and likewise exchanging the ת for ש produces the word קשר and reveals the **connection** in **Keter**. We have seen above (p. 91) that health depends upon the proper connection (קשר) among all parts of the soul and body, and we noted the equivalence of קשר (**connection**) and כשר (**fitness**).

---

refer to the **sefirot**: the י to **Chochmah**, the upper ה to **Binah**, the ו (with a **gematria** of 6) to either **Daat** or to the Six Emotional Attributes (**Chesed, Gevurah, Tiferet, Netzach, Hod, Yesod**), and the latter ה to **Malchut**. In this scheme, **Keter** is too sublime to be represented by a letter but is instead represented by the infinitesimal first point of the letter י. (This point of **Keter** is, in fact, the "source" from which each of the twenty-two Hebrew letters evolves, as is seen in the graphic form of each letter which evolves from such a point.)

Exchanging the ת for ש: The letter ת can be exchanged for ש, for many Aramaic words exchange a ת for the ש in their Hebrew counterparts. For example, the word שלש (three in Hebrew) is תלת in Aramaic. Other Hebrew-Aramaic pairs include ז-ד, צ-ט, ס-ש, צ-ע.

The essential relationship between light and health is seen in the connection between the word כתר and health. The **Baal HaTurim** states that the sum of the names of the letters of אור (*light*) is 623 – that is, the numerical value of 620 for the word כתר plus three, the value of one for each of the three letters of the word אור (light). This hints to the fact that **Keter** is the primal source of light as well as health.

Most interestingly, the numerical value of כתר, with the addition of one for the **kollel,** is three times the numerical value of אור (*light*). For כתר includes the three primary **sefirah**-attribute (also known in the Kabbalah as **lights**): **Wisdom (Chochmah), Understanding (Binah),** and **Knowledge (Daat)** which, according to the Kabbalah, are the source of all Creation. This is reflected in the numerical value of the phrase חכמה בינה ודעת (*Wisdom, Understanding,* and *Knowledge*) being equal to the numerical value of כתר.

---

*Baal HaTurim: Rav Yaakov ben Rav Asher of Toledo (approx. 5029-5100). (On **Parashat Yitro**.)*

א *is written* אלף: $1 + 30 + 80 = 111$

ו *is written* וו: $6 + 6 = 12$

ר *is written* רש: $200 + 300 = 500$

$$623 = 620 + 3$$

Three times the numerical value of אור:

כתר: $20 + 400 + 200 = 620 + 1 = 621$

אור: $1 + 6 + 200 = 207 \times 3 = 621$

Source of all Creation: Shlomo HaMelech alludes to this in

In the Kabbalah, another name for **Keter** is עתיק (**Atik**), meaning Ancient One [note the similarity to English "antique"]. In the Hebrew alphabet, the letters following its root letters (עתק) spell פאר (splendor).

א ב ג ד ה ו ז ח ט י כ ל מ נ ס **ע** פ צ **ק ר** ש **ת**

פ	follows	ע
א	follows	ת
ר	follows	ק

As we have seen, פאר is the spiritual source of health and healing. This again shows that health depends upon a Jew's connection with **Keter,** the Crown of Torah.

◇ ◇ ◇
◇

Proverbs (3:19-20): "G-d founded the earth with **wisdom,** established the heavens with **understanding.** Through His **knowledge** the depths were sundered, and the skies dripped dew."

Numerical value of . . . חכמה בינה ודעת:

חכמה	בינה	ודעת:
8+20+40+5	+ 2+10+50+5 +	6+4+70+400 = 620

כתר: 20 + 400 + 200 = 620

א *follows* ת*: The Torah is infinite, without end; the alphabet, therefore, is considered to be cyclical.*

chapter fifteen

THE 620 LIGHTS

T he Kabbalah speaks of the commandments (Scriptural and Rabbinic) as 620 Pillars of Lights. These lights compose the Crown of Torah and are the source of spiritual and physical health.

How so? The human body, state the Sages, parallels the 613 commandments; its 248 organs correspond to the 248 positive commandments, and its 365 sinews correspond to the 365 negative commandments. Since the commandments are to be performed by the physical body and, as stated above, the numerical value of the Hebrew word for lights (אורות) is 613, these "lights" are the underlying spiritual structure that gives life to the body's physical structure. It is not surprising, then, that good health depends upon the learning of Torah and the performance of the 613 commandments.

The connection between Torah, *mitzvot* (commandments), and health is discussed by the Talmud:

---

620 Pillars of Light: תרך עמודי אור. See **Kehilat Yaakov:** כתר.
The Talmud: **Berachot** 5a.

*R. Shimon ben Lakish said: Whoever oc-
cupies himself with Torah, sufferings
stay away from him. ... R. Yochanan
said to him: Even toddlers in school
know this, as is said: "And he said: If
you listen to the voice of G-d your
G-d, and do what is correct in His
eyes, and listen to His commandments,
and guard all His statutes, all the diseases that I put upon Egypt I shall not
put upon you, for I G-d am your doctor." Rava (and some say, R. Chisda)
said: If a person sees that sufferings
[i.e. sickness] have come upon him, he
should examine his deeds. ... If he ex-
amined [his deeds] and did not find
[any sin], he should attribute [the suf-
ferings] to neglect of Torah study.*

In this connection the Talmud stresses the importance of pronouncing the words of Torah that one is
studying:

*Shmuel said to R. Yehudah: Open your
mouth when you review. Open your
mouth when you read, so that [what
you study] will stay with you, and you*

And he said: If you listen: **Exodus** 15:26.
The Talmud: **Eruvin** 54a.

will live long, as it is said: "They are life for those who find them, and healing to all his flesh." Don't read "those who find them" [למצאיהם], read: "those who pronounce them aloud" [למוציאיהם]! ...

The word רפואה (**healing**) can be analyzed as made up of the two words אור (**light**) and פה (**mouth**). When the light of Torah is pronounced through the mouth, there is healing.

Our Talmud passage continues:

R. Yehoshua ben Levi said: If a person's head aches, he should engage in Torah-study, as it is said: "They are an adornment of graciousness [for your head]." If his throat hurts, he should engage in Torah-study, as it is said: "... and a necklace about your throat." If his stomach hurts, he should engage in Torah-study, as it is said: "It [fear of

---

They are life: כי חיים הם למצאיהם ולכל בשרו מרפא (**Proverbs** 4:22).

למוציאיהם: Literally, "for those bringing them out."

They are an adornment: כי לוית חן הם לראשך (**Proverbs** 1:9).

And a necklace about your throat: וענקים לגרגרתיך (**Proverbs** 1:9).

It [fear of G-d] is healing: רפאות תהי לשרך (**Proverbs** 3:8).

Navel: Ibn Ezra (to this verse) explains that the navel, the point through which the mother's blood enters the fetus, symbolizes the strength of the entire body, for the initial formation of all organs begins there.

G-d] is healing for your navel." If his bones hurt, he should engage in Torah-study, as it is said:"... and replenishment for your bones." If his whole body hurts, he should engage in Torah-study, as it is said: "... and healing to all his flesh." R. Yehudah bar R. Chiya said: Come and see that the way of the Holy One, Blessed is He, is not like the way of flesh and blood. When a human being gives a medicine to his fellow it is good for this [organ] but bad for that one. Not so is the Holy One, Blessed is He. He gave the Torah to Israel, and it is an elixir of life for man's whole body, as it is said: "... and healing to all his flesh"!

In the Talmud quoted above, the word for *healing* is רפאות. Its numerical value − 687 − equals the numerical value of two of G-d's names − א-ה-י-ה and י-ה-ו-ה − written in all their "full" forms. This is one of the hidden ways in which the Holy Tongue reveals that full awareness of G-d results in health.

---

*And replenishment for your bones: ושקוי לעצמותיך (**Proverbs** 3:8). The numerical value of רפאות:*

רפאות: 200 + 80 + 1 + 6 + 400 = 687

The human body consists of 248 organs . . .
248 positive commandments: That is, "You shall do . . ."
365 negative commandments: That is, "You shall not do . . ."
The name of G-d , א-ה-י-ה, can be written out in three ways:

אלף א	111		אלף א	111		אלף א	111
הי ה	15		הה ה	10		הא ה	6
יוד י	20		יוד י	20		יוד י	20
הי ה	15		הה ה	10		הא ה	6
	161			151			143

161 + 151 + 143 = 455

The Ineffable Name, י-ה-ו-ה, can be written out in four ways:

יוד י	20		יוד י	20		יוד י	20		יוד י	20
הי ה	15		הי ה	15		הה ה	10		הא ה	6
ויו ו	22		ואו ו	13		וו ו	12		ואו ו	13
הי ה	15		הי ה	15		הה ה	10		הא ה	6
	72			63			52			45

72 + 63 + 52 + 45 = 232
455 + 232 = 687

י-ה   has a numerical value of 15:
י-ה: 10 + 5   = 15

[P]ermutations of the Ineffable Name: The four letters of the Tetra-grammaton (י-ה-ו-ה) can be spelled out phonetically by means of the esoteric system of "filling" (מלוי, milui). Thus the first letter of the Name —י— can be depicted as יוד and as such be assigned the value of 20. Likewise is the first ה assigned the value of 6; the ו, 13; the second ה, also 6:

יוד: 10 + 6 + 4 = 20
הא: 5 + 1   = 6
ואו: 6 + 1 + 6 = 13
הא: 5 + 1   = 6
                          45

Each of the four permutations —עב, סג, מה, בן — corresponds to one of the letters of the Tetragrammaton as well as to one or more attributes of G-d as revealed through the sefirot. The name מה thus corresponds to the ו of the Four-Lettered Name and refers to the **sefirah** of תפארת and to the six (ו = 6) Emotional Attributes (מדות).

chapter sixteen

THE SOUL AND THE HEBREW ALPHABET

T he most fundamental level of Torah is the Hebrew letters. Thus, teaches R. Chaim Vital in the name of the *Arizal,* there is a definite spiritual connection between the soul and the healing powers of the Hebrew alphabet. The *Ravad* writes that the Hebrew alphabet is the foundation of the soul.

The Psalmist King David writes: "He forgives all your sins; He heals all your sicknesses." In this verse, forgiveness precedes healing. The verse contains twenty-seven letters corresponding to the twenty-seven letters of the Hebrew alphabet the twenty-two principal letters plus the five final forms. Healing, then, depends

---

R. Chaim Vital: See **Shaar HaMidah** *in* **Shaar HaKavanot.**

He forgives all your sins: הסלח לכל עו’נכי הרפא לכל תחלואיכי *(Psalms 103:3).*

The twenty-seven letters of the Hebrew alphabet: Interestingly, the number twenty-seven also represents purity, for this is the numerical value of the word זך*, meaning pure. As is known, tissue must be physically pure and uncompromised in order to heal. So too the soul.*

upon the Hebrew letters, the foundation of the Jewish soul.

Indeed, the eighth blessing of the **Shemoneh Esreh** prayer − *"Heal us, G-d, and we will be healed ..."* − is a request for both physical and spiritual well-being. Interestingly, this blessing comprises twenty-eight words. Twenty-eight is the numerical value of the Hebrew word כח, meaning **strength.** What is more, this blessing includes 120 letters, the number of years associated with full life, as was that of Moshe our teacher: *"And Moshe was a hundred and twenty years when he died."*

Though most letters of a Torah scroll are written in a uniform size, certain letters must be written especially large or small. Thus there are three sizes of letters in the Torah corresponding to three parts of the human soul: the small letters correspond to the **nefesh,** or animal soul, which vitalizes man's physical functions; the regular-sized letters correspond to the **ruach,** which is connected to emotional life; and the large letters correspond to the **neshamah,** man's link with the upper worlds and his connection to pure intellect and apprehension of the

Hebrew word כח:

כח: 20 + 8 = 28

"And Moses was a hundred and twenty years": ומשה בן מאה ועשרים שנה במתו. And as with the common Yiddish blessing: ביז הונדערט און צוואנציק: "[May you live] until a hundred and twenty!"

Divine. Examples of this graphic correspondence are as follows:

Large letters: **_neshamah_**   (example: **_Exodus_** 34:14)

Regular letters: **_ruach_**

Small letters: **_nefesh_**   (example: **_Leviticus_** 1:1 **_Ibid._** 6:1)

> *"All the souls that came with Yaakov into Egypt ... were sixty-six."*

In his writings on the science of reading the face, R. Chaim Vital teaches in the name of the **_Arizal_** that three rows of the Hebrew alphabet, corresponding to these three parts of the soul, can be seen on a person's forehead. The sixty-six souls of this verse are a hidden allusion to these three rows of principal letters of the alphabet.

Likewise, the twenty-seven letters of the Hebrew alphabet (the twenty-two principal letters plus the five final forms) may be divided into three groups of nine. Numerically, these three groups represent units of ones, tens, and hundreds and correspond to the Worlds of

---

All the souls: כל נפש ששים ושש . . . כל הנפש הבאה ליעקב מצרימה **(Genesis** 46:26).

The science of reading the face: חכמת הפרצוף **(chachmat hapartzuf)**.

Three rows of principal letters: 3 × 22 = 66.

The five final forms: צ, פ, נ, מ, כ have final forms used at word's end: ץ, ף, ן, ם, ך.

Asiyah (Action), *Yetzirah (Formation)*, and *Beriah* (*Creation*) as well as to the first three levels of the soul:

א-ט	1-9	ones	*Asiyah*	*nefesh*
י-צ	10-90	tens	*Yetzirah*	*ruach*
ק-ץ	100-900	hundreds	*Beriah*	*neshamah*

As is known, the number nine represents completion and perfection of a numerical series; there are nine numerals (not including the symbol 0) in the digital system and no more. Thus twenty-seven, or three times nine, represents perfection on all three of the levels shown above. As shown below, the number twenty-seven also represents purity (זך). Thus the twenty-seven letters of the Hebrew alphabet symbolize complete purification of these three levels.

The number twenty-seven as a symbol of completion is also revealed in the word הריון, *pregnancy*. Its numerical value is 271, representing the perfection of 27, in the three worlds and the three levels of the soul. Here

---

The number nine represents completion and perfection: The perfect truth of the number nine is seen in this number's unique ability to generate itself. As is known, all multiples of the number nine reduce to nine. That is, nine times any number will always equal a number whose digits add up to nine. For example, 9 × 5 = 45 (4 + 5 = 9); 9 × 17 = 153 (1 + 5 + 3 = 9). In fact, the Hebrew word for truth —אמת (emet) — illustrates this truth; its numerical value is 441 (א = 1, מ = 40, ת = 400) or, in reduced value, 9 (4 + 4 + 1).

The digital system: For example, when counting by units of one the highest possible value is 9. When counting by units of ten, the highest possible value is 90; by hundreds, 900, and so on.

the 27 is multiplied times ten, representing all ten of the
sefirah-attributes of creation, plus one to indicate the
One Source of all creation. This is another indication
that man's essence is based upon the twenty-seven letters of the Hebrew alphabet.

> *Another verse referring to healing is*
> ***Exodus*** *15:26: "He said: If you listen*
> *to the voice of G-d your God and do*
> *what is honest in His eyes and give ear*
> *to His commandments and guard all*
> *His statutes, I shall not put upon you*
> *all the diseases that I put upon Egypt;*
> *for I, G-d, am your healer"* ויאמר אם
> שמוע תשמע לקול ה' אלקיך והישר בעיניו
> תעשה והאזנת למצותיו ושמרת כל חוקיו כל
> המחלה אשר שמתי במצרים לא אשים עליך
> כי אני ה' רפאך.

This verse contains twenty-seven words, corresponding to the twenty-seven letters of the alphabet.
Moreover, it contains 110 letters. Adding one for the
verse as a whole, this gives 111. This is the numerical value of the name of the letter א when written out in full.

אלף: $1 + 30 + 80 = 111$

The letter א is the central letter of the word פאר
(***Splendor***). Its great importance for healing is explained
above (p. 60, sec. 6-8).

> *"Remove (הגו) the dross from the silver,*
> *and a vessel emerges for the refiner."*

As expounded upon above (p. 70), the Hebrew word הגו stems from the root הגה, meaning *to remove*; it contains the same letters as the word גהה, meaning *health*. The Hebrew word for dross is the plural סיגים; in the singular, סיג. Through the *At-Bash* transformation (see Introduction), סיג transforms to חמר, meaning *material*, a reference to materiality.

ס	transforms to	ח
י	transforms to	מ
ג	transforms to	ר

A person needs to remove the excess materiality (חמר) from himself. Then he will be pure (זך) and complete like the twenty-seven letters of the alphabet – fitting "vessels" to receive and transmit the Divine Light.

Remove the dross ... refiner: הגו סיגים מכסף ויצא לצרף כלי *(Proverbs 25:4).*

chapter seventeen

THE LIGHT OF THE MOUTH

W hy is the blessing of healing the eighth blessing in the ***Shemoneh Esrei*** prayer? The Talmud explains that it is because the ***brit milah*** (circumcision) is performed on the eighth day. The ***brit milah*** symbolizes purity, an essential requirement for healing. The number eight represents the supernatural, the numinous, that which transcends nature. In Kabbalah, the ***sefirah***-attribute corresponding to the ***brit milah*** is ***Yesod (Foundation)***. The word ***Yesod*** (יסוד) has the numerical value of eighty, which is ten times eight. As mentioned, the multiplication of a numerical value by ten indicates the full perfection of the

---

*The Talmud explains: (**Megillah** 17b).*

*The number eight represents the supernatural: For seven represents the order of the natural world, as is written: "In six days G-d made the heavens and the earth, the sea and all that is in them, and He rested on the seventh." (**Exodus** 20:11) Interestingly, the traditional double-looped symbol of infinity resembles the numeral eight lying on its side.*

יסוד has the numerical value of eighty:

יסוד: 10 + 60 + 6 + 4   = 80

quality of that number. Thus **Yesod** is the full perfection of the purity of the **brit milah.** This purity on the earthly level is represented by the number eight, and in a higher world by the number eighty.

As mentioned above, a Hebrew word for healing is רפואה which comprises the words אור and פה, **light** and **mouth,** indicating the important role of pure, holy speech in healing. This is also connected with the purity of the **brit milah,** for the numerical value of מילה is the same as that of פה. As the Sages state: *"Life and death are in the power of the tongue."*

◇ ◇ ◇
◇

The numerical value of מילה is . . . that of פה:

מילה: 40 + 10 + 30 + 5 = 85

פה: 80 + 5   = 85

chapter eighteen

FOUR FOURS: TORAH, G-D'S NAME, MAN'S SOUL, AND MAN'S BODY

I n the Evening Prayer, just before reciting the ***She-ma,*** appears the blessing אהבת עולם ("Eternal love"). The principal theme of this prayer is Torah-study. As such, this blessing reveals the link between the Torah and man's body and soul and further clarifies why spiritual and physical health depend upon learning and living in harmony with the Torah.

The blessing begins: *"With eternal love You have loved Your people, the House of Israel. You have taught us*

With eternal love: אהבת עולם בית ישראל עמך אהבת ,תורה ומצות חקים ומשפטים אותנו למדת.

It is interesting to note that the blessing אהבת עולם *begins with the Hebrew word for love (*אהבה*):*

With eternal love You have loved Your people . . .

This word is actually a form of the Ineffable Name of G-d . Its first letter א, *as written in a Torah scroll in the scriptstyle as detailed by R. Yitzchak Luria, consists of three letters: a* י *above, a central* ו, *and a* ד *below. Thus is spelled* יוד *(yud), the name of the letter* י. *The word's second letter* ב *is pronounced as is the letter* ו *and is*

Torah and commandments, decrees, and laws..." The blessing subsequently mentions four aspects of Torah Law – *Torah* (תורה), *commandments* (מצות), *decrees* (חוקים), and *laws* (משפטים) which correspond, states the Kabbalah, to four aspects of man's soul: *chayah, neshamah, ruach,* and *nefesh.*

The highest of these four aspects of the soul is called חיה (*chayah*), meaning *living.* It corresponds to *Torah* (תורה), which is the source of all life, as is written: *"It is a tree of life for those who hold onto it."*

The next aspect of the soul is called נשמה (*neshamah*), from the Hebrew root נשם, meaning *breath.* This is the soul-aspect that links the upper worlds with

---

therefore interchangeable with it. By exchanging the א for י and the ב for אהבה, ו becomes י-ה-ו-ה, the Ineffable Name.

Moreover, the numerical value of the Name is exactly twice that of אהבה:

י-ה-ו-ה: 10 + 5 + 6 + 5 = 26

אהבה: 1 + 5 + 2 + 5 = 13

And thus is the message of this blessing. By giving us the four aspects of the Torah, which correspond to the four letters of His Name, G-d gives us, as it were, His own Name (י-ה-ו-ה), which is love (אהבה). The Torah is G-d 's will, the expression of G-d 's love for the Jewish people — a true and eternal love.

Chayah, neshamah, ruach, and **nefesh**: נפש, רוח, נשמה, חיה. The fifth and most sublime aspect of the soul, the **yechidah** (יחידה), transcends the four soul-aspects, which are listed here in decreasing order of sublimity.

It is a tree of life: עץ חיים היא למחזיקים בה (**Proverbs** 3:18).

the lower worlds. It corresponds to the **commandments** (**mitzvot**), which unite the upper worlds with the lower worlds; through the commandments the will of Heaven is realized on earth, and through the performance of the commandments man establishes his link with G-d.

The second highest of these aspects of the soul is called רוח, literally **wind** or **spirit**. It involves the emotions which motivate man, turbulent and changeable like wind. The primary resting place of this aspect of the soul is the heart, the seat of the emotions, and it corresponds to the **decrees** (חוקים). An allusion to this is seen in the Hebrew alphabet: the letter following ק in the alphabet is ר. Exchanging ק for ר, the word חוק (**statute**) becomes חור (**hole**), the same letters as רוח. The word חוק comes from a root meaning **to carve out,**

---

*The soul-aspect that links: The root of the word **mitzvah** (מצוה) means **attachment**: With the fulfillment of each **mitzvah** man attains the greatest good of human life — attachment to G-d Himself. For it says in the fourth of the **Chapters of the Fathers**: "The reward for a **mitzvah** is a **mitzvah**." That the commandments effect attachment to G-d Himself is seen clearly in the very word itself. On one level, the Hebrew word for commandment (מצוה) is the simple nominal form stemming from the root צוה, meaning **attachment** (a related word צות means **crew** — a group united by a common task). However, by means of the **At-Bash** transformation, the letters מצ transform to the letters י-ה; the word מצוה, therefore, transforms to the Ineffable Name, י-ה-ו-ה — a clear allusion to the connecting power of G-d's commandments.*

*decrees (חוקים) : Examples of decrees are the commandment to prepare the Red Heifer (**Numbers 19:2**) and the injunction not to wear a mixture of wool and linen (**Deuteronomy 22:11**). Their un-*

to hollow out, or *to engrave.* Thus in meaning, as well as form, חוק is close to חור. As is seen, חור has the same letters as רוח – the soul-aspect which resides in the heart. The heart is a hollowed organ, consisting of four main "holes" or chambers, and the heart's physical task is to circulate blood through the blood vessels, which too are hollow. Physically, this hollowness is essential to the body, to the free circulation of the blood. When the "holes" are open and unobstructed, the heart can perform unencumbered. So too with man, whose spirit (רוח) must also be "open" to receive and feel, to be sensitive

---

derstanding is at present beyond human comprehension; these statues are to be fulfilled at this time by simple adherence to G-d 's will as revealed in the Torah. Yet while fulfilling the commandment, the Jew, says the **Rambam,** is free to speculate, to conjecture as to what could be the Divine intention.

When the "holes" are open and unobstructed: Awareness of the great gift of bodily wholeness is the intention of the blessing אשר יצר *(asher yatzar,* "Who has formed ..."), said after elimination:

> Blessed are You, L-rd our G-d , King of the universe, Who has formed man in wisdom, and created within him numerous orifices and cavities. It is revealed and known before the Throne of Your Glory that if but one of them were to be blocked, or one of them were to be opened, it would be impossible to exist even for a short while. Blessed are You L-rd, Who heals all flesh and performs miracles.

Why should the blessing for bodily health include a declaration that G-d "performs miracles"? The answer is that man himself is a miracle, for the nature of his soul is to flee the body and return to its supernal source; the nature of his body is to return to the earth

to the needs of others and most importantly to G-d's will.

The next aspect of the soul is called *nefesh,* related to a root meaning *to want* or *to desire.* This is the lowest, most earthly aspect of the soul; it corresponds to the *laws (mishpatim),* the civil and ritual laws pertaining to worldly matters.

The numerical value of *law* (משפט) is 429. With the addition of the *kollel* (1), the result is 430 — the numerical value of *nefesh* (נפש). As mentioned above, the addition of the *kollel* to a word so that it may equal another word illustrates the spiritual dependence of the first word on the second word of larger numerical value; that is, the second word represents the spiritual source of the first. Here, משפט (*law*) is the spiritual source that

---

(אדמה, *adamah) from which it was brought forth, as is written: "Then the L-rd G-d formed the man (Adam) of dust of the ground" (Genesis 2:7). It is solely through G-d 's miraculous intervention that the union of human soul and body is made and sustained.*

Meaning to want: Compare the Aramaic אפש (efesh) meaning desire; and Rashi to Genesis 23:8: נפשכם (" 'Your nefesh' [means] your will.").

mishpatim: Examples of laws are more numerous than decrees. They include the commandment to leave uncut a corner of one's field for the poor (Leviticus 19:10) and the prohibition not to tattoo the skin (Leviticus 19:28).

The numerical value of law (משפט)...the numerical value of נפש:

משפט: $40 + 300 + 80 + 9 = 429$

נפש: $50 + 80 + 300 = 430$

sustains man's *nefesh,* his animal soul. These civil laws provide the framework of civilization needed to control and order man's earthly desires stemming from his *nefesh.*

These four parts of the soul also correspond to the four letters of G-d's name: י-ה-ו-ה. The highest of the four parts of the soul, the *chayah,* corresponds to the first letter of G-d's Name, the י. The *neshamah* corresponds to the first ה; the *ruach* to the ו; and the *nefesh,* the most earthly part of the soul, to the final ה, which symbolizes G-d's kingship on earth.

The four main parts of the human body also correspond to the Ineffable Name of G-d. The head corresponds to the first י; the abdomen, arms, and hands correspond to the first ה; the lower center of the body, including the womb and the reproductive organs, to the ו; and the thighs, legs, and feet to the final ה. In fact, this is seen in the very shape of these letters:

י

An elevated point, the י is the only letter set off from the baseline on which all other Hebrew letters rest or traverse. So too the head, the highest portion of the human body; it is elevated both in its position and in its purpose in the body;

The first ה

The letter of breadth and breath, the ה extends both horizontally and vertically, like the abdomen, the principal extension of the human body; in addition, the ה is called "A light letter without substance" – the principal letter of unvocalized breath;

ו
_____

The letter of downward extension, the ו represents the lower body and, specifically, the male reproductive organ; and

The final ה

Balanced and stable, the ה graphically symbolizes the support given by man's lower extremities – his thighs, legs, and feet.

This, spiritually and physically, is the image of G-d in which man is created. It is this spiritual and physical creation (the union of soul and body) that reflects the Name of G-d and which man can perfect and keep healthy by learning and fulfilling all four parts of the Torah: *"Torah and commandments, statutes, and laws."*

Indeed, man's dual nature, spiritual and physical, is

[The letter ה is] the letter of breadth and breath: See **Igeret HaTeshuvah** *by R. Schneur Zalman of Liadi, Ch. 4.*

A light letter without substance: אתא קלילא דלית בה מששותא *(See* **Akdamut,** *the traditional Aramaic hymn recited on Shavuot, the Festival of Weeks).*

*The image of G-d in which man is created: For it is written (***Genesis** *1:26):* נעשה אדם בצלמנו כדמותנו *("Let us make man in Our image, after Our likeness.").*

alluded to in the Torah's account of Creation. In reference to the creation of the animals and birds, the Torah
uses the term יצר (*He made*). In reference to the
creation of man, the Torah uses the same term, but
spells it וייצר – with two י's, an allusion to man's spiritual
soul and physical body.

Man's physical body comprises four elements: earth,
air, fire, and water. His soul comprises four levels:
chayah, neshamah, ruach, and *nefesh,* plus the
yechidah which, referred to as "the supernal mystery,"
transcends the four other soul-levels. This dual make-
up, physical and spiritual, is reflected in the word for
man: אדם. The work *Shem MiShmuel* points out that the
letter ד has the numerical value of four, referring to the
above-mentioned four elements. The letter ם, it states,
has the numerical value of forty, which is ten times four.
As is known, multiplying a value by ten indicates that it
is parallel, but on a higher spiritual level. Thus the מ
refers to the four upper elements – these four levels of
the soul. The letter א, whose numerical value is one,
refers to the *yechidah,* for this word means *singular,* a
true *one* with no second. Thus, says *Shem MiShmuel,*
the word אדם shows man's essential physical and
spiritual components and their relation to each other:

יצר: (*Genesis 2:19*).
וייצר: (*Genesis 2:7*)

the four lower elements (ד), the four upper elements (מ), and the *yechidah* (א) above them all.

chapter nineteen

ABRAHAM AND HEALING

T he Patriarch Avraham (Abraham), the point of origin of Judaism, was also an all-inclusive source of healing. The Talmud states:

> R. Shimon ben Yochai says: "A jewel hung at the throat of our father Avraham. Any sick person who saw it was immediately healed. When our father Avraham died, the Holy One, Blessed is He, took [this jewel] and hung it upon the sun." Abbaye said: "This is the meaning of the folk saying: 'When the sun lifts up, the sickness lifts off" (**Bava Basra** 16b, as cited in **Ein Yaakov.**)

Rashba (quoted by **Ein Yaakov**) explains that the jewel symbolizes wisdom. Avraham transmitted his wisdom to many students. The jewel is said to have hung at his throat, the part of the body that emits speech, because he communicated his wisdom by speaking. In this way, says **Rashba,** Avraham brought his disciples under the protective wings of the Divine Presence, healing them in body and soul.

Avraham's connection with healing is hinted in his name, אברהם, which can be analyzed as אבר מה. The first part, אבר means *limb* or *organ.* The second part, מה, has the numerical value 45; it represents the permutation of the Name of G-d which includes the letter א and is equal to this value (see above, p. 124). As seen above (p. 60), the letter א stands for wisdom. The word פאר, which denotes the spiritual root of healing (see above, p. 50) also has the numerical value 45 through the *Al-bam* (אל-בם) transformation (see Introduction). Thus the name Avraham can be read as the *"limb or organ of the source of healing."*

chapter twenty

HALO, AURA AND SHADOW

An interesting aspect of the relationship between light, air, and health is the concept of the halo or aura. [Note the similarity between Heb. אורה, *orah, light,* and Engl. *aura.*] Both are defined as an appearance of light surrounding the body. The quality and color of the light is an indicator of the body's health.

The concept of health as connected with light that surrounds the body is expressed in the structure of the Hebrew word אבר, meaning *limb* or *organ.* This word can be analyzed as the letters אר surrounding the letter ב. The letters אר are the basic letters of the word אור (*light*) while the letter ב represents the concept of house or physical structure (the name of the letter *bet* itself – בית – means *house* or *structure*). The body is the physical structure that houses man's soul which is compared to light. [Note the similarity of "body" and "abode."] For any limb or organ to be complete and sound, this physi-

---

*Halo or aura: Compare the English **halo** to the Hebrew הילה (**hila**) meaning **halo** or **halation.***

cal structure must radiate and be surrounded by light. Only then is it worthy of the name אבר.

The Hebrew word for health – בריאות – contains the letters of בית (house) surrounding those of אור (light). When the edifice of the body is surrounded by light, the result is health. Likewise, when health is present the body is full of light.

As is man's aura, so too is man's shadow. One a light and the other the absence thereof, both are ethereal visual phenomena surrounding the body and reflecting its condition. Moreover, the shadow is produced by light. When there is no source of light, there is no shadow.

When Joshua encouraged the Children of Israel not to fear the Canaanites, he assured them: *"Their shadow has departed from upon them."* Based on this and the verse in **Song of Songs** exhorting, *"until ... the shadows have fled,"* the Kabbalah states that one's shadow departs thirty days before death. The **Zohar** explains that darkened portions in a person's aura indicate sickness in a corresponding part of the body.

The Code of Jewish Law mentions that if one wishes

Their shadow has departed: סר צלם מעליהם (**Numbers** 14:9).
Until . . . the shadows have fled: (2:17) עד . . . ונסו הצללים.
*The Kabbalah states: (**Zohar,** end of **Beshalach**).*
The Code of Jewish Law: **Shulchan Aruch** (664:1).

to know whether he will live during the coming year, he should look to see if his body casts a shadow in the moonlight on Hoshana Rabba, the seventh day of *Sukkot,* the Festival of Tabernacles. This custom is no longer practiced, for the technique of observing the shadow is no longer known. Hence the practice might lead to unnecessary worry, which in itself is dangerous to health.

Indeed, fear and worry damage the body. This is evident from analyzing the word פחד, meaning *fear.* It consists of פח plus ד. The first part, פח, means *a snare;* the second is the letter ד, whose numerical value is four, alluding to the four elements composing the physical body: earth, air, fire, and water. Thus fear (פחד) is a snare (פח) of destruction for the health of the body (ד). A similar message is conveyed by the root חרד, which denotes *trembling fear.* This word can be analyzed as חר plus ד. The first part, חר, is the root of the word חור, *hole.* The ד, as stated, stands for the physical body. Like a sword (חרב), which tears a *hole* (חר) in the physical "housing" (ב) (see below, p. 160), so too *trembling fear* (חרד) makes a *hole* (חר) in the physical body (ד). Analysis of the root רעד *(to tremble)* reinforces this understanding. This root consists of רע *(bad)* plus ד. Again we see that trembling and trepidation are bad (רע) for the body (ד).

Still, from the very fact that this moon-shadow technique was once used, we learn that the state of health is reflected in the phenomenon of light surrounding the body.

The concept underlying the halo, aura, or shadow is that the physical body depends upon its spiritual base or environment. Job commented on this when he said: *"From my flesh I see G-d"*; that is, that the physical body actually reflects spiritual reality. This is expressed in the words אומר (*he says*) and חומר (*material*). The word אומר represents man's spiritual nature, which is manifest most basically in the human ability to verbalize thoughts. The word אומר begins with the letter א representing G-d and the study of the Divine will (see above, p. 60). The word חומר, on the other hand, begins with the letter ח, which represents physicality. Both are produced in the back of the throat; the sound of א is so ethereal that it is usually not pronounced at all, while the sound of ח is strong and rasping.

The health of the physical body can be the result of one's spiritual condition. Physical health depends upon spiritual health. This is represented by the concept of the halo, aura, and shadow, which provide a visual image of the spiritual "body" encompassing the physical body. So of course the condition of the halo, aura, or shadow reveals the condition of one's health.

"From my flesh I see G-d ": ומבשרי אחזה אלוה *(Job 19:26).*

chapter twenty-one

THE EFFECT OF THE SPIRIT ON THE BODY

Sometimes the physical result of a spiritual state is immediate. The Talmud relates the story of the siege of Jerusalem, when Rabban Yochanan ben Zakkai had himself smuggled out of the city and brought before the Roman general, Vespasian.

> *Rabban Yochanan said: "Greetings, O King!" Vespasian replied: "You have made yourself liable to the death penalty ... [for] I am not the king, and you called me king."*
>
> *Rabban Yochanan said: "You are undoubtedly a king, for if you were not a king, Jerusalem could not be given over into your hand."*

And with this Rabban Yochanan proved his contention from Scripture. The narrative continues:

*The Talmud relates: (**Gittin** 56a).*

Just then an emissary arrived from Rome and informed Vespasian that the emperor had died and that Vespasian had been appointed as his successor. At that moment, Vespasian had a shoe on one foot. When he tried to put on his other shoe, he could not. When he tried to remove the shoe that was already on his foot, he could not do that either. He exclaimed, "What is this?"

[Rabban Yochanan] told him: "Do not be distressed. You have just received good news, and Scripture says: `Good news fattens the bones.' "

"But what is the remedy?"

"Bring someone with whom you are dissatisfied, and have him walk in front of you, for it is written: `A depressed spirit dries the bones.' "

Vespasian followed this advice. When his mood was soured by seeing someone he disliked, his foot returned to normal size and he was able to remove the shoe.

This is an outstanding example of the principle that one's spiritual condition influences one's physical condition – the basic principle of psychosomatic medicine.

Good news fattens: שמועה טובה תדשן עצם *(Proverbs 15:30).*
A depressed spirit: ורוח נכאה תיבש גרם *(Proverbs 17:22).*

King Solomon stressed this when he said: *"A man's spirit strengthens him in his sickness, but who will lift up a broken spirit?"* Explains the **Malbim**:

> *It is the spirit that sustains the body. And even if there is sickness in the body, the spirit has great enough strength to support the illness, giving the person strength to bear [the illness] and renew his courage. But if the spirit is broken – referring to spiritual sickness – who will lift it up? For then the sickness will affect the body, too, as it is written: "A depressed spirit dries the bones."*

And **Metzudat David** comments:

> *But when the spirit itself is broken by sadness and depression, who will lift it up? For the body does not lift it up to strengthen it; rather, it is the spirit that supports the body.*

In short, spiritual health is the source of physical health, and not the contrary.

A man's spirit strengthens: רוח איש יכלכל מחלהו ורוח נכאה מי ישאנה *(Proverbs 18:14).*
Malbim: R. Meir Leibush ben Yechiel Michel.
*Physical health is not the source of spiritual health: Indeed, Shlomo HaMelech states in **Proverbs** 17:22: "A happy heart makes for good health." But as Maimonides states in **Hilchot Deot** 4:1, physical health is a prerequisite for spiritual effort but a healthy body does not in itself produce a healthy spirit.*

The most insidious of spiritual illnesses is depression; in Hebrew, דכאון. The root of this word is דכא – meaning *to crush* or *to humble* – may be seen as דך א. The word דך means *poor, crushed, humbled.* And as stated above (see p. 152), the letter א refers to the Divine, to man's spiritual essence – his ability, his yearning to transcend the physical to connect with his Creator. As such, the rightful place of the א is at the fore, in the leading, dominant position of the root, as in אדם, the very word for spiritual man. In דכא, however, the א is delegated to the root's end, dominated by the letters דכ. So, too, in depression is man's spirit and G-dly aspirations crushed and humbled.

The numerical value of דכאון is 81 – the same numerical value as טבע, the Hebrew word for *nature.* And so we learn: When one forsakes one's spiritual pleasures for his baser natural pleasures, depression can result. To be happy means to be spiritually healthy; to be spiritually healthy, a person's spiritual will must control his natural desires.

The letters following דכא in the Hebrew alphabet are הבל, which means *vanity, nothingness.* When one is involved in materiality, in empty, vain matters, he falls

---

The numerical value of טבע . . . דכאון . . . is 81:

דכאון: 4 + 20 + 1 + 6 + 50 = 81

טבע: 9 + 2 + 70   = 81

into depression and perceives his existence as הבל, a fleeting, empty thing.

The effect of depression on the body is seen when we read the letters of דכא in reverse. They spell אך ד. The first part, אך (literally, "*but, however*") is a word indicating exclusion – i.e. it indicates that something is eliminated or reduced. The second part, ד, as we saw above, stands for the four elements, the foundation of physical existence. Depression diminishes the body's physical existence.

chapter twenty-two

THE EAR — GATEWAY TO THE BODY

An interesting approach to healing, and one that is practiced with proven results, is called auricular healing. It is based on the concept that the human ear is a model for the entire body. The practitioner of auricular healing diagnoses the source of disease by examining the patient's ear, and treats the disease by inserting needles into the appropriate parts of the ear. *Midrash Rabbah* speaks of the centrality of the ear to the rest of the body, and at the same time reveals the spiritual basis of this relationship. First, the Midrash discusses the spiritual importance of the ear:

> *Our Rabbis said: Do you wish not to have pains in your ear nor in any of your limbs? Then bend your ear to Torah, and you will inherit life, as it is said: "Incline your ear and go to Me; listen, and give life to your soul."*

Midrash Rabbah (Deuteronomy, parashah 10): האזן לגוף כקנקל לכלים.

Afterwards, the Midrash is more explicit in describing the centrality of the ear to the other organs. It compares the ear to an implement called a *kinkal,* an inverted, perforated vessel in which incense was burned. Items of clothing were hung above it, the scent wafting through the holes and perfuming the garments.

> *R. Levi said: The ear is to the body as the* ***kinkal*** *is to the clothes. A number of garments are placed over the* ***kinkal,*** *and you put incense under it, and all of them become scented. Likewise, all the 248 limbs of man live by means of the ear. How do we know? Because it is said: "Listen, and give life to your soul."*

Apparently, this spiritual relationship has its physical parallel, as utilized by auricular healing.

Interestingly, through the analysis of the word פאר (see above, p. 50) is seen how the quality of balance is crucial to health. The Hebrew word for ear אזן has the same three-letter root as the word אזן, meaning *balance.* Physiologically, too, man's ability to actually maintain physical balance depends upon the health of the *mal-*

Incline your ear: הטו אזנכם ולכו אלי שמעו ותחי נפשכם *(Isaiah 55:3).*
Kinkal: *In Hebrew,* קנקל.

leus, incus, and *stapes* – the three miniscule bones located in the inner ear.

The relationship between פאר, the spiritual source of the qualities of balance and harmony, and the word אזן is further revealed in the full spelling of the names of the letters אזן. The sum of these names is equal to the numerical value of פאר, plus three for each of its three letters.

What is more, the letters that spell אזן can be analyzed as א plus זן. As mentioned, the letter א represents the Divine, and also man's ability to learn the Divine will. The word זן means *to feed* and *to nourish.* As such the ear is the opening through which knowledge of the Divine is fed into the body, giving it and the soul spiritual nourishment and thereby creating the balanced state of health.

A similar idea is alluded to by the fact that the

Malleus, incus, and *stapes:* Commonly referred to as the *mallet, the anvil,* and the *stirrup.*

Full spelling of the names of the letters אזן:

א: אלף: *1 + 30 + 80* = *111*

ז: זין: *7 + 10 + 50* = *67*

ן: נון: *50 + 6 + 50* = *106*
   284

Numerical value of פאר:

פאר: *80 + 1 + 200 = 281 + 3* = *284*

The first such appearance of the letter נ: *(Genesis 1:20).*

word אזן is also an acronym for the phrase אלף זנה נפש, meaning "[The letter] *alef* nourishes the soul." The Sages say that the essential meaning of a letter is indicated by its first appearance in the Torah in a significant position in a word (for example, as the first letter of the word). (See **Pri Tzaddik** by R. Tzaddok Hakohen, beginning of **Genesis**.) The first such appearance of the letter נ is in the word נפש, meaning *soul*. Hence the letter נ represents the soul in this acronym. Here, too, we see that the ear is the channel of sustenance for the soul. This idea is also seen in the fact that the numerical value of האזנה (*to give ear, to listen*) is equal to that of חיים (*life*).

When we look at the letters that precede אזן in the alphabet, we find תום, meaning *perfection*.

ת precedes א (The alphabet is considered to be cyclical.)

ו	precedes	ז
ם	precedes	ן

Perfection means that all the necessary components of an entity are present, balancing each other in the right proportion. This is the quality that charactizes Yaakov (Jacob), who is called איש תם *"a perfect man"* (see above, p. 114). This perfection is the underlying source of balance (אזן), for which a key organ is the ear (אזן).

Because of this vital function of the ear and the faculty of hearing, the verb שמח, *to rejoice* is closely related to שמע, *to hear.* (The letters ע and ח are inter-changeable since both are gutteral, that is, produced with the back of the throat.) Hearing causes happiness – especially hearing the truth about G-d's will. And *"A happy heart improves the health"* (**Proverbs** 17:22).

The word שמח (to rejoice) can be analyzed as ש plus מח. The first letter, ש, represents light. This letter has three "flames" emanating from its base. According to the **Arizal,** the one on the right has the form of the letter ו; the middle one has the form of a י; and the one on the left, the form of a ז. Thus the three "flames" spell the word זיו, meaning **shining radiance.** The remaining two letters spell מח (brain). When a person is happy, his brain is filled with light. [It is interesting to note that the Chinese word for "soul" is *shen.* Compare also English *shine* and *sheen.* (For the connection between light and health, see above, p. 117).

Tikunei Zohar points out that the word meaning thought, which is spelled מחשבה contains the same letters as בשמחה, meaning *in joy.* Man's purpose in life is to *"Serve G-d in joy"* (עבדו את ד בשמחה) (**Psalms** 100:2). Through thought, we increase our ability to serve G-d joyfully. And through being in a state of joy we strengthen our power of thought.

The numerical value of מחשבה (*thought*) is 355, which equals that of ספירה, *sefirah,* a kabbalistic term denoting one of the ten basic channels of spiritual emana-tion through which G-d creates and sustains the world.

This same number, 355, is also the numerical value of the phrase שם י-ה, meaning *the name of G-d*. From this we learn that man's power of thought (מחשבה) is closely connected to the basic creative forces emanating from the Holy One, Blessed is He. Through these creative forces the name of G-d is revealed in the world.

This is one of the reasons why man is called אדם (*adam*). The Sages point to the similarity of אדם to אדמה (*adameh*), which means *I resemble*. In the tremendous creative potential of his power to think, man can humbly and gratefully declare: *"I resemble the Supernal One"* (אדמה לעליון; *Isaiah* 14:14).

chapter twenty-three

A HEALING HEART

The relationship between spiritual and physical health is highlighted by King Solomon: *"A healing heart is life for the flesh; but anger is rot for the bones"* (חיי בשרים לב מרפא ורקב עצמות קנאה; ***Proverbs*** 14:30). Ibn Ezra explains that a "healing heart" means *"a heart that does not get angry and does not envy others."* It is called this because *"it is like medicine for the body... a good, happy heart heals the body by means of its joy."*

Malbim explains why this is: *"The life of the flesh – and its healing if it becomes weak – depends upon the heart. When the heart is brave and strong, it sends out [the blood] to course through the blood-vessels in swift-flowing streams that nourish and give life to the body. Therefore, if someone blocks his heart with anger, he not only destroys the flesh, but even rots the bones and ruins the body. Thus, it is written: 'Above all, guard your heart, for from it are the outpourings of life'* (מכל משמר נצר לבך כי ממנו תוצאות חיים; ***Proverbs*** 4:23).*"*

The above verse refers particularly to the rotting of the bones, because the bones are the most essential part of the physical structure. Thus, regarding the wish, *"May*

He strengthen your bones" the Talmud says that this is: *"The best of blessings"* (*Yevamot* 102b).

The word for *rot* in this verse is רקב. It can be analyzed as: רק plus ב. The first part, רק, are the basic letters of the word, ריק, *empty.* The second part, the letter ב, represents the *house* (בית). Thus, *rot* means "an empty house," a dwelling that is devoid of content. Good *midos* (character traits), such as joy and appreciation, produce spiritual light. But if the body, which is the house or dwelling-place of the soul, is devoid of light and faith, the result is physical degeneration, i.e., *rot.* (See above).

Similarly, the word חרב, *sword,* consists of חר plus ב. The letters חר are the basis of the word חור, *hole.* The sword has the destructive power to make a hole in the house (ב) of the body. The Sages refer to harmful foods as being "like swords (חרבות) to the body" (see below, p. 207).

Another example of the relationship between spiritual and physical health is the fact that anger has a deleterious effect on eyesight. King David said: *"My eye deteriorated from anger"*(עששה מכעס עיני; *Psalms* 6:8). The emotion of anger arises from the liver, as the Sages said: *"The liver gets angry"* (כבד כעס; *Berachot* 61b).

Further insight into this connection between the eyes, the liver, and anger is found in *Sefer Yetzirah,* which shows how the constellations correspond to parts of the body. Capricorn corresponds to the liver. The moral attribute of Capricorn is anger. It was created with the letter ע, whose name (עין) means *eye.*

Chinese medicine also notes the connection between the eye and the liver. This explains why jaundice, a disease of the liver, reveals itself in the eyes (the whites of the eyes turn yellow).

The connection between the liver and anger is reflected in the English language, where someone who is irritable is said to have a "jaundiced" disposition, or to be "bilious." In fact the word "bile" has two meanings: (1) the fluid produced by the liver; (2) anger.

In Hebrew, the word for *anger* is כעס, which can be analyzed as כס ע. The first part, כס, means *to cover,* while the second part, ע, means *the eye.* Thus *anger* means "covering the eye." Both spiritually and physically, it destroys one's ability to accurately perceive his surroundings.

This is further revealed through the letters that follow כעס in the Hebrew alphabet. They are עפל, a root related to אפל, meaning *darkness.* Anger darkens one's eyes. עפל also means a fortification or barrier, hinting that anger isolates a person and creates a barrier between him and others.

Another root meaning *to be angry* is רגז. The same letters in different order spell גזר, which means *to cut off.* Here too we see the destructive outcome of anger and its effect of separating people from each other and from their Creator.

In the Hebrew alphabet the letters following רגז are שחד, meaning *bribery*. This teaches us that anger destroys a person's objectivity. Here too there is a hint of anger's debilitating effect on eyesight, as it is written:" כי השחד יעוור עיני חכמים *As bribery blinds the eyes of the wise ones. (Deuteronomy 16:19).*

chapter twenty-four

FAITH, THE BASIS OF GOOD CHARACTER

The source of good character traits is faith – אמונה. This word can be analyzed as: א plus מונה. The first part, the letter א, stands for the Divine, and for man's ability to learn and contemplate (see above, p. 60). The second part spells מונה, meaning *to count*, i.e., to take account of something, to attach importance to it. (We count things that are precious to us; a significant thing "counts.") Thus faith, אמונה, means to take account of the Divine; to give importance to it and think about it.

Traits like anger and jealousy come from a lack of faith. This is expressed by ***Proverbs*** 16:28: *"The complainer separates the leader [from the people]"* (ונרגן מפריד אלוף). The word for *leader* is אלוף. Its root is אלף, which is also the name of the letter א. Thus the verse can be read: 'The complainer drives away the א.' A negative attitude drives out the א, which is the essence of אמונה, faith.

A similar idea is embodied in the word, עצב, *sadness,* which consists of the letter צ wedged in between the letters עב. The letter צ (*tzaddi*) symbolizes the righteous one (*tzaddik*), while עב means **thick**. Thus sadness is a state in which awareness of G-d, the Righteous One, is repressed and smothered as if by a thick covering. Or to put it another way, the righteousness (*tzaddik*) within a person is closed in and covered over.

This is a destructive situation, as can be seen in the fact that the letters of עצב, in different order, spell בצע, which means **to cut, break**. In the Hebrew alphabet the letters preceding those of עצב and בצע are אפס, which means **zero, nothing**. Sadness breaks and cuts a person, reducing him to nothingness. By analyzing the word אפס we discover the reason for this. This word consists of א and פס. As we have seen, א stands for אמונה, **faith**. The letters פס are a root meaning **to cease,** as in the verse: *"Faithful ones have ceased* (פסו) *from among mankind"* (פסו אמונים מבני אדם; *Psalms* 12:2). Thus אפס can be seen as "cessation of faith." When faith ceases (אפס), there is danger of sadness (עצב), which destroys (בצע) physical health.

If the letter ב in בצע is replaced by פ (these letters are interchangeable because they are both labials), the result is פצע, **to wound.**

Hiding the light and joy of righteousness causes destruction. For this reason, the word סתר has a double meaning. It signifies both **to hide** and **to demolish.** [Note the similarity between Heb. סתר, **satar** and Engl. **store,** meaning to hide away, and also Engl. **destroy** and **shatter.**]

"My son, do not forget My Torah, and let your heart guard My commandments. For they will add to you length of days, years of life, and peace" (בני תורתי אל תשכח ומצותי יצר לבך כי ארך ימים ושנות חיים ושלום יוסיפו לך; *Proverbs* 3:1-2). Wisdom is life. The word for "length" in this verse is ארך, which can be seen as אר כ, where אר means *light* and כ stands for *crown,* כתר.

The Gemara in its analysis of the alphabet – *Shabbos* 104a – says that the letter כ stands for the crown that the Holy One, Blessed is He will place on the heads of the righteous in the world to come. According to *Kehilat Yaakov,* another word that refers to the Crown is קרן (*Keren*). This word signifies the horn of an animal, or a ray of light. We find it as a verb in the Torah's description of Moses when he descended from Mt. Sinai: *"The skin of his face radiated"* (קרן עור פניו; *Exodus* 34:29). A horn is like a crown because both radiate from the head. [The English word "crown" is phonetically similar to *keren* ("horn"); both have the same three consonant sounds in the same order: *k. r. n.*

In Kabbalah, the *Crown (Keter)* is the highest of all the spiritual realms, or *sefirah*-attributes that are the channels of creation. By learning Torah and becoming wise, one draws down upon himself the beneficient, life-giving light of the *Crown.* One of the words for *healing* is ארוכה. This word, too, contains אור כ, *the light of the Crown.* Learning the wisdom of the Torah, and obeying its commandments, brings healing through the light of the *Crown.* The *Crown* is the highest source of creation of which man can know anything at all. Health means being attached to the source. Through Torah-study, one becomes attached to the source.

chapter twenty-five

TORAH, THE ONLY EFFECTIVE REMEDY

Referring to Israel's exile, the Torah says: *"When many troublesome evils overtake [the nation]"* (כי תמצאן אתו רעות רבות וצרות; *Deuteronomy* 31:21). The Talmud says: *"What [is the meaning of] 'troublesome evils?' Rav said: '[It means] evils that are troublesome to each other, such as [the sting of] the wasp and the scorpion'"* (*Chagigah* 5a). *Tosafos* explains this in the light of the Gemara which states that someone who has been stung by a scorpion needs to be warmed up, while someone who has been stung by a wasp needs to be cooled off (*Avodah Zarah* 28b). Hence if someone is stung by both these creatures, he cannot be cured. The remedy of each sting is "troublesome" to the other.

One could say that this imagery symbolizes the spiritual illness of exile, i.e., of being distant from G-d. A person becomes "cold" and indifferent to the performance of the *mitzvot*; therefore he needs to be warmed up. But at the same time he is "hot" in pursuit of the appetites and urges of the evil inclination; therefore he needs to be cooled off. Apparently there is no remedy for this situation. Whatever is good for him is also bad for him. This in fact is the fear expressed by R' Yochanan: *"A servant whose master produces for him 'troublesome evils' – is there any remedy for him?"* The answer would seem to be that there is only one medicine that can cure this type of illness, and that medicine is Torah, which is *"healing to all his flesh"* – ולכל בשרו מרפא (*Proverbs* 4:22). This is the advice the Talmud gives. *"R' Elazar's disciples asked him: 'What can a person do to be saved from the birth-pangs of Mashiach?'* [He answered:] *'Let him engage in learning Torah and doing kindness to others'"* (*Sanhedrin 108b*).

The holy **Zohar** points out that the word רע (*evil*) when written in reverse spells ער, meaning **awake, alert** [compare ער, *er,* with Engl. "aware"], teaching that the purpose of the so-called "evils" is to awaken people and help them repent.

chapter twenty-six

THE CONNECTION BETWEEN SOUL AND BODY

T he healing power of Torah and *mitzvot* stems from the fact that the *mitzvot* (commandments) constitute man's spiritual body. As mentioned above, R' Chaim Vital teaches that the 365 negative commandments correspond to the 365 sinews of the physical body, while the 248 positive commandments correspond to the 248 organs. Thus it is written: *"From my flesh I see G-d"* (ומבשרי אחזה אלוק; *Job* 19:26). Through the 613 parts of the physical body, one can see the spiritual body that was created in the image of G-d. This is the connection between body and soul, on the level of the *mitzvot.*

The power of the *mitzvot* to bring unity between body and soul, and between man and God, is revealed in the number 613, the number of Scriptural commandments in the Torah. This is the total of the numerical value of the two words, *connection,* קשר (600) and *one,* אחד (13). Moreover, when we add together the digits of 613 (6 + 1 + 3), the total is ten, the number that stands for completion and perfection. Through the 613 *mitz-*

vot, a person connects himself with his soul and with his Creator on all ten dimensions of existence.

The component numbers of 613 – 1, 3, 6 – form a harmonious chord in the musical scale; see our work **Music and Kabbalah.**

On the level of Torah-study, the Jew's most basic obligation is to recite the **Shema** *("Hear, O Israel...")* twice daily. The full form of the **Shema** consists of three paragraphs from the Torah. Their 248 words correspond to the 248 organs of the human body (see **Shulchan Aruch, Orach Chaim** 61:3). Each word of the **Shema** gives life to a particular limb. This is one important connection between body and soul on the level of Torah-study.

Another connection on the level of Torah-study is explained by R. Tzaddok Hakohen (in **Pri Tzaddik, Parashat Toldot**). He says that the word *tent* (אהל, *ohel*) signifies the spiritual "tent" of light that surrounds the physical body.

[It is interesting to note the correspondence between the English word *halo* and Hebrew *ohel.* The letters of the English alphabet correspond in both form and sound to those of the Hebrew alphabet. (This is because the English alphabet is derived from the Roman alphabet, which in turn is derived from Hebrew; see our work, **Hebrew: Source of Language.**)

h	corresponds	to ה
a	corresponds	to א
l	corresponds	to ל
o	corresponds to the vowel	*cholam.*

Thus *halo* corresponds to אהל (*ohel*), *tent.*]

The numerical value of אהל is 36. This corresponds to the 36 times the word "light" (in various forms) appears in the Torah. This hints that the light of the Torah is man's spiritual tent.

The first letter of אהל is א, whose name, *alef,* also means *a thousand.* If we count the א as 1,000, the numerical value of אהל is 1035. This is five times the numerical value of the word, *light* (אור). 5 × 207 = 1035. In the account of Creation (*Genesis* 1:1-5), the word *light* appears five times. This is a hint that man's spiritual covering, his "tent," consists of five levels of light, corresponding to the Five Books of Moses. These five levels are the five parts of the soul.

The highest level is called יחידה (*yechidah*), which means literally, *single one.* It corresponds to the Book of *Genesis,* which tells of the lives of the Patriarchs, who are called the "single ones" of the world.

The next level is called חיה (*chayah*), meaning *alive.* It corresponds to the Book of *Exodus,* for it tells of the giving of the Torah, which is the source of life.

The next level is called נשמה (*neshamah*), *breath.* It corresponds to the Book of *Leviticus,* which speaks of the sacrifices. The sacrifices are the link between the upper and lower worlds. Similarly, the *neshamah* is the link between the spirit and the body. It resides in the brain (*mo'ach*), the part of the body that performs the spiritual function of reasoning.

The next level is called רוח (*ruach*), meaning, **wind** or **spirit**. It is nearer to the physical level of existence and corresponds to the Book of **Numbers,** which tells of the physical life of Israel in the wilderness.

The lowest level of the soul is called נפש (*nefesh*), which is the physical life-force of the body. It corresponds to the Book of **Deuteronomy.** This Book consists of a review of the entire Torah in preparation to enter the Land of Israel, where the life of the nation would enter a more earthly, physical phase.

The relationship between the parts of the soul and the books of the Torah is tabulated as follows:

yechidah	Genesis
chayah	Exodus
neshamah	Leviticus
ruach	Numbers
nefesh	Deuteronomy

The two highest levels of the soul, **yechidah** and **chayah,** are known as "tents," because they are outside and above the body. This shows another connection between our forefather Yaakov (Jacob) and healing, for Yaakov is referred to as the one who "sits in tents" (see above, p. 44).

These relationships have recently been reinforced by computer analyses of the Torah (see the works of Drs. Katz and Witztum, such as המימד הנוסף and באותיותיה נתנה תורה; their work is based on the findings of R. Weismendel in תורת חסד). R. Weismendel began with the first letter ת in the Book of **Genesis** and counted forty-nine letters. He found that the fiftieth letter is ו. Carrying on in the same way, he found that the next fiftieth letter is ר, and the next, ה. This spells תורה, Torah.

The exact same pattern was found in the Book of **Exodus**.

In the Book of **Leviticus**, beginning from the first י in the Book, and taking every eighth letter, he found that the letters spelled י-ה-ו-ה, the ineffable name of G-d.

In the Book of **Numbers**, beginning from the first ה in the Book and taking every fiftieth letter, he found the word תורה (Torah) written in reverse. And this exact same pattern was found in the Book of **Deuteronomy**.

Why is the word **Torah** encoded in normal order in the Books of **Genesis** and **Exodus**, but reversed in the Books of **Numbers** and **Deuteronomy?** The answer is that, as we have just seen, the first two books correspond to the two highest parts of the soul, the **yechidah** and **chayah**. Their function is to bring light down from the higher worlds to the lower. This is the "normal" order, in which the higher influences the lower. Therefore in these Books the word **Torah** is written in "normal" order. On the other hand, the Books of **Numbers** and **Deuteronomy** correspond to the lower parts of the soul, the **ruach** and **nefesh**. Their function is to raise up earthly things to a higher, more spiritual level. This is the reverse of the "normal" order, and therefore in these Books the word **Torah** is written in reverse order.

All this spiritual work – of bringing down light from above and raising the material world to a more spiritual level – is performed with the help of the *neshamah,* which occupies the middle position and serves as the link between the upper and lower worlds. For this reason the letters of *neshamah* (נשמה) are the same as those of *shemoneh* (שמנה), which means *eight.* This number represents the connection between the lower and upper worlds, for it follows the number seven, the number that represents the totality of the natural world (as in the seven days of the week). [The number eight, drawn as if lying on its side, is the mathematical symbol for infinity.] Thus the number eight consists of an upper and a lower circle, symbolizing the upper and lower worlds. It is appropriate, then, that the ineffable name of G-d is encoded in the Book of *Leviticus* (*neshamah*) through every *eighth* letter.

In summary: Man's spiritual body corresponds to his physical body on the level of the *mitzvot,* on the level of the *Shema,* and on the level of The Five Books of Moses. By connecting himself with the Torah, a person builds and strengthens the "tent" (*ohel*) of light that surrounds and protects him.

Sefer Yetzirah, an ancient work of Kabbalah (attributed to the Patriarch Abraham) gives a system of correspondences that connects man's physical body not only with his spiritual qualities, but also with other basic features of Creation. It states that each month of the year is associated with a particular one of the Twelve

Tribes, a sign of the Zodiac, a letter of the Hebrew alphabet, a character trait, and a part of the body.

For example, the month of Teves is associated with the Tribe of Dan, the sign of Capricorn, the letter ע, the trait of anger, and the liver. The name Dan is derived from the word דין (*din*), which means *strict judgment.* To execute strict judgment, one must use the trait of anger. As we saw above, the liver is the physical organ connected to the spiritual trait of anger.

Another link between the physical body, the spiritual body, and the cycle of time is revealed by the holy *Zohar (Parashas Vayishlach)*, which states that each of the 365 negative commandments is connected to a particular day of the year and an organ of the body. Someone who violates that commandment causes damage to that day of the year and that organ. For example, the ninth of Av (Tisha B'Av) is connected with the sciatic vein (*gid hanasheh*). The *Zohar* finds a hint of this in the verse, *"Therefore to this day the children of Israel do not eat the sciatic vein"* (על כן לא יאכלו בני ישראל את גיד הנשה; *Genesis* 32:32), where the term גיד הנשה is preceded by the word את, whose letters form the initials of אב תשעה, meaning "Av nine," the ninth of Av. The commentaries also say that the term for the sciatic nerve, *gid hanasheh* (גיד הנשה) is an allusion to *gid hanashim* (גיד הנשים), meaning literally "the organ of women," that is, the procreative organ. This means that this day of the year (Tisha B'Av) and part of the body

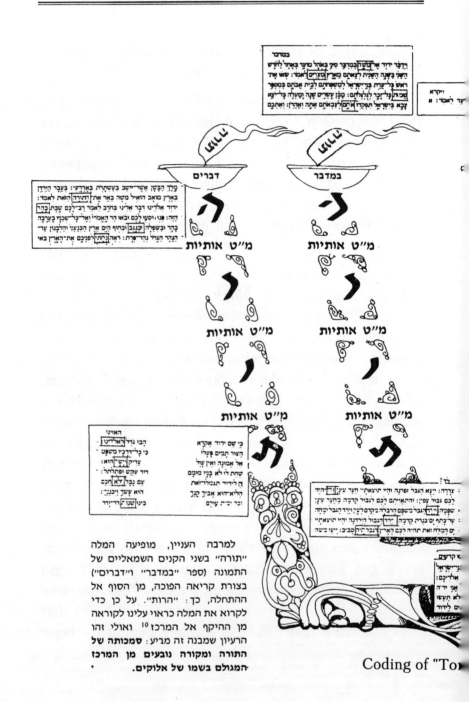

למרבה העניין, מופיעה המלה "תורה" בשני הקנים השמאליים של התמונה (ספר "במדבר" ו"דברים") בצורת קריאה הפוכה, מן הסוף אל ההתחלה, כך: "הרותי". על כן כדי לקרוא את המלה כראוי עלינו לקוראה מן ההיקף אל המרכז [10] ואולי זהו הרעיון שמבנה זה מביע: **סמכותה של התורה ומקורה נובעים מן המרכז המגולם בשמו של אלוקים.**

Coding of "To

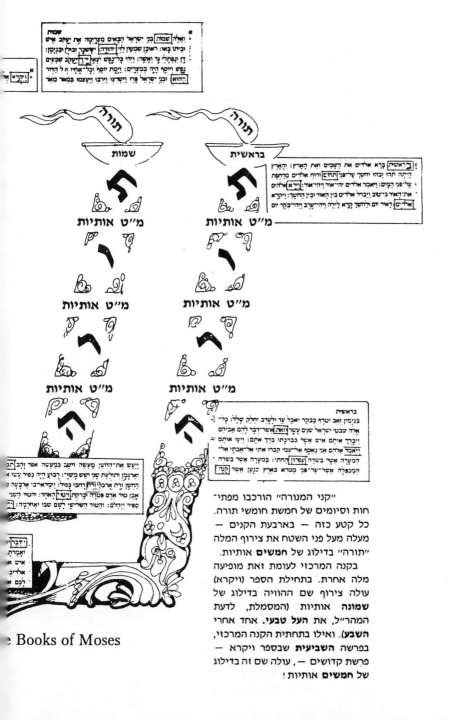

e Books of Moses

"קני המנורה" הורכבו מפתי־
חות וסיומים של חמשת חומשי תורה.
כל קטע כזה — בארבעת הקנים —
מעלה מעל פני השטח את צירוף המלה
"תורה" בדילוג של **חמשים** אותיות.

בקנה המרכזי לעומת זאת מופיעה
מלה אחרת. בתחילת הספר (ויקרא)
עולה צירוף שם ההוויה בדילוג של
שמונה אותיות (המסמלת, לדעת
המהר"ל, את **העל טבעי**. אחד אחרי
השבע). ואילו בתחתית הקנה המרכזי,
בפרשה **השביעית** שבספר ויקרא —
פרשת קדושים — , עולה שם זה בדילוג
של **חמשים** אותיות!

(the sciatic vein) are especially connected with the task of sanctifying man's procreative urge.

This is another aspect of the connection between man's spiritual body and his physical body. It gives us a deeper insight into the concept of psychosomatic medicine and shows why spritual perfection, i.e., full observance of the Torah, is the basis of physical health.

chapter twenty-seven

FEAR AND WORRY — ENEMIES OF HEALTH

Health depends on fear of God. This is shown by the fact that the word for *healthy* is ברִיא, which contains the letters of ירא, meaning *he fears*. Likewise, the feminine form of the word *healthy* is בריאה, which contains the letters of יראה, meaning *fear*. (There are several words for "fear" in Hebrew, but יראה connotes fear of something high or distant. The unqualified term יראה, *yir'ah,* is understood to mean fear of God.) King Solomon says: *"Fear of G-d adds length of life "* (יראת ה' תוסיף ימים; *Proverbs* 10:27).

The word ביראה, meaning *for fear* contains the same letters as בריאה, which means Creation. This underlines the principle that the purpose of Creation is that man should fear G-d.

The letters of יראה also spell ראיה, which means *seeing.* Fear of God means to keep Him always before one's eyes, as it is said: *"I place G-d in front of me always"* (שויתי ה' לנגדי תמיד; *Psalms* 16:8; and see *Shulchan Aruch, Orach Chaim* 1:1). Unlike fear of man, which causes depression and is harmful to health, fear of

God causes joy and is good for the body, as we see from the continuation of that verse in **Psalms**: "Therefore my heart rejoices...my flesh, too, dwells securely" (לכן שמח אף בשרי ישכן לבטח...לבי; ibid. v. 9). When a person fears God, he does not fear other things, and is free of health-destroying worry.

The letters of יראה in different order spell ריאה, **lung**. The lungs contain air, the essence of life. Without this restrictive framework, the air would dissipate and life would be impossible. Similarly, fear of G-d provides the framework of self-discipline that enables a person to use his creative powers in constructive, life-giving ways.

While fear of G-d is the basis of life, fear about worldly matters is destructive to life. The Talmud says: "Three things take away a person's strength: fear, travelling, and sin" (**Gittin** 70a). As we saw above (p. 146) worldly fear, פחד, is a snare (פח) of destruction for the four elements (ד) that comprise the body. From another viewpoint, fear is a sign that one is trapped in the snare (פח) of materialism, the world of the four elements (ד).

If a person is to be healthy, it is important that the aspect of materialism should be under the control of the spiritual aspect. This can be seen in the words הוד and דוה, which have the same letters but in different order. In הוד, which means **glory,** the predominant letters are הו. These are the two central letters of G-d's name (י-ה-ו-ה). They stand in their proper order, and in control of the four elements of materiality (ד) and hence G-d's glory shines forth. By contrast, in the word דוה,

which means *to be ill,* the ח is in the leading position. The letters וה are in reverse order and are under the control of materialism. The result is sickness.

The root that means *to worry* is דאג. It has the same letters as אגד, which means to bind things together. However, in אגד the letters are in proper sequence, following the order of the alphabet, while in דאג, *worry,* the letters are, so to speak, in distorted order.

In אגד, the first and hence predominant letter is א, which stands for the divine and for man's connection with the divine (see above, p. 60). The next two letters show the result of the divine impetus. They are גד. The Talmud (*Shabbat* 104a) says that these two letters, in this order, represent the man of kindness who strides toward the poor man in order to benefit him. That is, ג, whose shape suggests a leg extended forward, is the initial letter of גמילות חסדים (*gemilut chassadim*), which means "doing kindness," while ד is the initial of דל (*dal*), meaning "poor." Thus אגד (*agad*), the force that binds together all the members of society, represents divine influence causing people to do acts of kindness towards each other.

By contrast, in the word for *worry,* דאג, the first and dominant letter is the ד which stands for poverty. The א, or divine influence, which should be dominant, is instead trapped between the ד and ג. This symbolizes a situation in which the feeling of poverty is predominant, making a person feel he cannot afford to give to others.

— 181 —

It is interesting to note that these same relationships hold when we transliterate certain English words into Hebrew letters. The word **G-d** would be transliterated גד, showing the right relationship between the giver and the poor. On the other hand, **dog** would be transliterated דג. Here the relationship is reversed. Instead of the giver pursuing the needy, the needy pursues the giver. This is the image of the dog, an animal that is always looking for gifts.

The Sages say that the expression ויהי (**vayehi**), which means literally: "*And it shall be*," sounds like a cry of distress (**Voy!**), and whenever the Torah uses this expression it is hinting that the events described were troublesome (see **Shemos Rabbah** 20:7 et al.). From this we can learn that bringing the future into the present causes trouble. The antidote to fear and worry is to be relaxed (רגוע). The root of this word is רגע, which is also the root of רגע, meaning **a minute.** When one focuses on the present, one minute at a time, he can relax.

From the above examples, as revealed in the profundities of the Hebrew language, it is clear that positive or negative spiritual and emotional states produce corresponding effects on one's physical health.

chapter twenty-eight

THE STRENGTH OF THE TEETH

An example of the connection between the physical and the spiritual body is seen in our teeth. The teeth represent man's strength. After death, they last longer than the rest of the body. Just as the soul is the strongest, most enduring part of man in his entirety, so the teeth are the strongest, most enduring part of the physical body. Hence the tooth symbolizes the soul. Thus when King David speaks of the complete destruction of the enemy, he says: *"You have broken the teeth of the wicked"* (שני רשעים שברת; *Psalms* 3:8), and *Rashi* explains that "teeth" means "their strength."

There are thirty-two *"Pathways of Wisdom"* (*Netivot Hachochmah*) in the Torah, corresponding to the thirty-two exegetical principles of expounding the Torah, as taught by R. Eliezer the son of R. Yossi Hagelili (in a *baraisa* printed at the end of Tractate *Berachos*). Applying these principles is the first step in "digesting" the wisdom of the Torah. Similarly an adult has thirty-two teeth, with which he breaks down his physical food, this being the first step in digestion.

chapter twenty-nine

THE WAR OF OPPOSITES

God created this opposite that" (זה לעמת זה עשה האלקים; *Ecclsiastes* 7:14). For every positive force, He created a corresponding negative force. This can be seen especially clearly in the letter ח. It is the initial letter of a group of negative words: חטא (*sin*), חולי (*sickness*), חומר (*material*), חול (*secular,* חילול (*desecration*), חולשה (*weakness*). This group of words shows us some of the qualities associated with sickness.

However, a number of positive words also begin with ח: for example, חיים (*life*), חידוש (*renewal, innovation*), חכמה (*wisdom*).

According to the **Arizal,** this diametric nature of the universe is symbolized by the very form of the letter ח. In a Torah scroll, this letter is composed of two letters ז, connected by a "roof." The name of the letter ז (*zayin*) means *weapon.* Hence the form of the letter ח suggests two opposing forces facing each other with weapons. Since ח stands for *life* (חיים), this teaches that life is a war between man's two inclinations, the Good Inclination and the Evil Inclination. If a person is to be healthy, these two forces must be in proper balance, with the Good Inclination dominant. If the Evil Inclination is too strong, of course the result is sickness. But the Evil Inclination cannot be ignored or repressed. It's strength, too, must be enlisted for positive purposes. There must be a constructive confrontation with the negative, and the tension of this confrontation is life.

The Torah says: *"You shall love the Lord, your God, with all your heart"* (ואהבת את ה' אלקיך בכל לבבך; *De-uteronomy* 6:5). The ordinary word for **heart** is לב, but in this verse the word used has the letter ב twice instead of once: לבב. The Sages expound this as meaning that one must serve G-d *"with both your inclinations, the Good Inclination and the Evil Inclination"* (**Berachot** 54a). The task of the healer is to help a person achieve the right balance of forces within himself, and to constructively utilize the bad forces as well as the good. This is represented by the symbol of the medical profession, the staff with the two opposing snakes (for more regarding the snake as a symbol of healing see above, p. 83).

This principle is also hinted at by the numerical value of רופא (*he heals*), which is 287. This equals the combined numerical value of the words for **good** and **ad,** טוב and רע.

רופא:	200 + 6 + 80 + 1	= 287
טוב:	9 + 6 + 2	= 17
רע:	200 + 70	= 270
		287

This teaches that even the bad within us has a purpose and can be used for constructive ends. True healing helps us utilize all our inner forces, both the good and the apparently bad. This enables us to serve G-d *"with both your inclinations."*

The word התרופה, which means *the cure,* has the numerical value 696. [Note the similarity between Hebrew תרופה, *terufah* and Engl. *therapy.*] This is also the numerical value of the word רצות, which means *to find favor, to be reconciled, forgiven.* Arranged in different order, the letters of רצות spell צרות, which means *troubles.* [Note the similarity between Heb. צרה, *tzarah* and Engl. *sorrow.*]

התרופה: 5 + 400 + 200 + 6 + 80 + 5 = 696

צרות or רצות: 90 + 200 + 6 + 400 = 696

According to the Kabbalah, *the cure* refers to repentance, as in the verse, *"He will repent, and will be cured"* (ושב ורפא לו; *Isaiah* 6:10). The fact that the above three words all have the same numerical value teaches that the power of repentance can change the *troubles* (צרות), which come as punishment for sins, into *favor* (רצות). This is an example of how bad is utilized and transformed into good.

The Torah commentary *Be'er Moshe (Parashat Balak)* says that the power of the righteous person, the *tzaddik,* is to change *trouble* (צרה) into *favor* (רצה) and *brightness* (צהר). He says that the *tzaddik* changes a decree of punishment (*trouble*) by rearranging the letters of the decree, e.g., by moving the letter צ so that צרה becomes רצה.

[This is similar to the transformation of *sickness* (דוה) into *glory* (הוד), mentioned above (p. 180).]

In the *At-bash* (את-בש) transformation, the letter corresponding to ח is ס (*samech*). By this same transformation, חטא, which means *sin,* becomes סתן (Satan), meaning the *Accuser* or the *Tempter.* The function of the Accuser is to surround a person, closing him off from the possibilities of life. This is symbolized by the round, closed shape of the letter ס.

The ס is another letter that reveals the dual nature of the universe as a battleground between good and evil. On the negative side, it is the initial letter of סתן or סטן (*Satan*), which means the *Accuser.* [The English letter corresponding to ס is "s." It too is the initial of many negative words, such as *sick, sin, secular, snake,* and *Satan.*]

On the positive side, ס is the initial of the word סמך (samach), which means *to support.* (This is also the name of this letter.) When people are supportive of each other, this creates joy, the prime emotional basis of health. Thus the letters of *samach, to support,* are identical in pronunciation to the letters of שמח (*samach*), which means *to rejoice.*

Those who specialize in computerized deciphering of the "codes" of the Torah have discovered that the disease known as Aids is encoded in the story of Sodom and Gomorra. Names, even the names of new diseases, are not coincidental. On the verse, "Go and see the actions of G-d, Who puts desolation on the earth" (לכו חזו מפעלות ה' אשר שם שמות בארץ; *Psalms* 46:9), the Sages comment: "Do not read "desolation" (*shamos*), but "names" (*shemos*)," meaning that Providence causes the appropriate name to be given to each person or thing. The word "Aids" in Hebrew is איידס, which can be analyzed as אייד (*eid*), "destruction," plus the letter ס (*samech*), whose name means "support." Aids is the destruction of the immune system, which supports and guards the cells of the body. (This can be seen in the shape of the ס, a closed circle representing a protective wall.)

Sodom and Gomorra were infamous for sexual immorality, which is a factor in the spread of Aids. The opposite of such immorality is the covenant of circumcision. The numerical value of איידס (Aids) is equal to that of מילה (*milah*), "circumcision."

איידס: 1 + 4 + 10 + 10 + 60   = 85

מילה: 40 + 10 + 30 + 5   = 85

The letter ש has two forms, one with a dot at the left (*sin*) and one with a dot at the right (*shin*). R. Akiva teaches that the form with the dot at the left (*sin*) symbolizes the negative forces, while the one with the dot at the right (*shin*) symbolizes the positive forces (*Otiot DeRabbi Akiva*) – "this opposite that."

מכלה בהם, ההיי"ו   הזהום   הרוס ○   החיסון   אידס ⬚

Coding of Aids in story of Sodom and Gomorah
from **Hameimad Hanosaf,** by **Doron Witztum**

ר ח ב י ח א ־ ב
ר ב י א ח ׳ א ח
א ׳ ם ם ר ב א א
ח ם א ר ׳ א ח ב
ר א ר ח ק ׳ ׳ ק
ם ב ר ם ר ח ח ר
ב ר ר ׳ א ח ח א
ם ח ם ב ב א ׳ ׳
א א ב ב ם ר ב ב
ר ר ר ׳ א ז ם ח
ר א ם ר ק ר ׳ ׳
׳ ר ׳ ם ׳ ח ח ח
׳ ׳ ר ב ם ר ב ח
ם ח ח ח ר א ׳ ר
ז ר ם א ר ב א ח
א ר ר ר ם ר ׳ ר
ר ׳ ם ק ׳ ׳ ר ר
ח ר ק ח ר ח א א
ב ר ח ׳ ב ר ר ר
ם ר ר ב ם ח ׳ ׳
ב ר ח א ׳ ר ם ק
ב ז ח ם ם ר ב ח
ר ׳ ׳ ר ר ח ם ר
ר א ח ׳ ׳ ח ב ר
׳ א ח ר ח ר א ב
א ר ח א ח א ח ר
ם ׳ ק ר א ר ר ח
ר ח ׳ ק ז ח ר ר
ר ר ח ב ר ר ם ח
א ר ר ם ב ח א ׳
א ח ח ר ר ר ר ר
ב ר ח ח ׳ ח ז ר
ם ב א ח ם ב ר א
׳ ר ב ׳ ר ר ר ם
ק א ר ר א ר ח א
ח ק ר ח ר א ח ׳
ב ם ח ח ר ק ח ח
ח ר ח ר א א ר ח

chapter thirty

BREAD IN THE MORNING

(PAT SHACHARIT)

"And it shall be, as a result of your listening to these laws, and keeping them and doing them . . . G-d will remove from you all disease" (והיה עקב תשמעון את המשפטים האלה ושמרתם ועשיתם אתם ... והסיר ה׳ ממך כל חלי; *Deuteronomy 7:12, 15).*

On this the Sages explain:

*[What is meant by "all disease?"] R. Elazar said: This is bile (**marah**). [**Rashi:** For the bitterness of it is intense, and it flows and spreads through the veins and bones.]*

[A baraisa] teaches the same: [Regarding the verse,

"You shall serve the Lord your G-d . . . and I shall remove sickness from your midst" (ועבדתם את ה׳ אלקיכם . . .

והסרתי מחלה מקרבך; *Exodus* 25:23),
the baraisa says:]

"[The word] 'sickness' means bile. And why is it
called 'sickness?' Because it sickens a person's entire
body. Another reason is: eighty-three diseases result
from bile – for this [83] is the *gematria* of מחלה
(*sickness*) – and all [these diseases] are annulled by
[eating] bread in the morning with salt, with a dipper of
water [*Rashi*: for someone who does not have wine]."

As *Rashi* notes, the fact that eating bread in the
morning annuls all these diseases is derived below from
verses. The Talmud now cites a second baraisa:

"Our Rabbis taught: Thirteen powers are attributed
to *pat shacharit* [bread in the morning]: It saves [a per-
son] from the sun's heat; from the cold; from winds; and
from demons; it makes the simple-minded wise [*Rashi*:
for his mind is settled, because he is not suffering from
pains (of hunger)]. One [who adopts the practice of eating *pat shacharit*] wins his law-cases [*Rashi*: if one must
go to court against someone, his mind will be settled so
that he can order his words in court to explain his
claims]; it helps him to study Torah and to teach it
[*Rashi*: because of his settled mind]; his words are hee-
ded [*Rashi*: people listen to him, since he has intelligence
(lit., heart) to explain]; what he learns stays with him; his
flesh does not give off an odor [*Rashi*: of sweat and dirt];
he has a healthy relationship with his wife and does not
desire other women; and [*pat shacharit*] kills parasitic
infestation of the intestines. And some add: it removes

jealousy [**Rashi**: for when a person does not feel satisfied, he is easily angered] and fills him with love."

Rabbah said to Rava bar Mari: What is the origin of the folk saying: "Sixty run hard but do not overtake the man who eats bread in the morning?" And our Rabbis said: "In summertime, eat early because of the heat; and in the wintertime, because of the cold." [Rava bar Mari] answered: [The source is] the following verse: "They shall not be hungry or thirsty; nor shall the heat or the sun smite them" (לא ירעבו ולא יצמאו ולא יכם שרב ושמש; **Isaiah** 49:10). [It informs us that] the heat and sun will not smite them, because they will not be hungry or thirsty. [Rabbah] countered: You say to me [that it is derived] from [that verse], but I say to you from [this verse]: "You shall serve the Lord your G-d and He will bless your bread and your water" (ועבדתם את ה׳ אלקיכם וברך את לחמך ואת מימיך; **Exodus** 23:25). "You shall serve the Lord your G-d" – this refers to the recitation of the **Shema** ['Hear O Israel...'] as well as the prayers; ". . . and He will bless your bread and your water" – this refers to bread and salt, with a dipper of water. Once a person has eaten this, then [the rest of the above verse] follows: "I shall remove sickness from your midst."

(*Bava Metzia* 107b and *Bava Kamma* 92b)

Note: The numerical value of פת (*pat,* "bread") is equal to that of תלמוד (*talmud*), which means "Torah study."

פת: 80 + 400   = 480
תלמוד: 400 + 30 + 40 + 6 + 4   = 480

This hints that Torah-study is the basic nourishment of the soul, as bread is the basic nourishment of the body.

OUR SAGES
ON
HEALTH

PREFACE

Following are some sayings of the Sages on the topic of health. (The author wishes to acknowledge the work: Otzar Musarei Chazal, by R' Aharon Yosef Barzel (Jerusalem, 5750) for the list of references.)

This section contains many remedies and treatments for a variety of sicknesses. The commentators have pointed out that in our time and age, when people's physical constitution and environment is not the same as in Talmudic times, not all such remedies are applicable for practical use. Nevertheless, one can glean from these sayings of the Sages many valuable principles and insights.

1. Rava bar Shmuel said in the name of R' Chiya: After every time you eat, eat salt, and after every time you drink, drink water, and you will not be harmed.

(Berachos 40a.)

2. It is taught [in a Baraisa]: If one ate any kind of food and did not eat salt, or drank any kind of beverage and did not drink water, he will have to be concerned about bad breath during the day and croup during the night.

(Ibid.)

3. The Sages taught: If one floats one's food in water [***Rashi***: drinks a lot of water after eating, to the point that his food floats in water], he will not have intestinal disorders. And how much [water should he drink to do this]? Rav Chisda said: a ladle to a loaf of bread.

(Ibid.)

4. Rav Mari said that Rabbi Yochanan said: One who is accustomed to [eat] lentils once every thirty days keeps the croup out of his home [***Rashi***: because sickness comes from constipation, and lentils promote elimination]. But [one should] not [eat them] every day. Why? Because that would cause bad breath.

(Ibid.)

5. Rav Mari also said that Rabbi Yochanan said: One who is accustomed to [eat] mustard once every thirty days keeps diseases out of his home. But [one should] not [eat them] every day. Why? Because that would cause weakness of the heart.

(Ibid.)

6. Rav Chiya bar Ashi said that Rav said: One who is accustomed to [eat] small fish will not get intestinal disorders. What is more, small fish cause a person to be fruitful and multiply, and they make his entire body healthy.

(Ibid.)

7. That which is near the soul [the source of vitality] restores the soul [restores one's vitality]. Rav Acha bar Yaakov said: [This refers to] *unka* [*Rashi*: the throat, which is where slaughtering is performed, and which is near the heart and the intestines]. Rava told his servant: When you get me a steak, take the trouble to get it from near the place of the blessing [*Rashi*: the place where the blessing over slaughtering was recited] – [i.e., the throat].

(Ibid. 44b.)

8. Rav Idi bar Avin said that Rav Yitzchak bar Ashian said: If one wishes to regain health, he should cut an olive's-bulk (*kezayit*) of meat from the place on

an animal where slaughtering is performed [i.e., the throat], salt it very well [to kasher it], rinse off [the salt and blood] very well [and eat the meat].

(Chullin 33a.)

9. Rav Acha said: One who goes to [a medical practitioner] should say: May it be Your will, Hashem, my God, that this action will result in healing for me and that You will heal me, for you are God, the reliable Healer, and Your healing is true; for it is not the way of human beings to heal [**Rashi**: that is, they should not have taken up healing, but should pray for mercy], but they have taken it upon themselves.

Abbaye said: A person should not say that [i.e., one should not say that human beings should not have taken up healing], for the yeshivah of Rabbi Yishmael taught [regarding the verse]: *"[If...one man strikes another...] he shall heal [him]"* (וכי...רעהו את איש והכה...ורפא ירפא; *Exodus* 21:18-19): "From this [we learn] that doctors have been given permission [from Heaven] to heal."

When one gets up [to leave the place of treatment] what should he say? Rav Acha said: Blessed is He Who heals without charge.

(Berachot 60a.)

According to the Gaon of Vilna, in the prayer on entering the doctor's office, instead of: *"... for you are*

God, the reliable Healer..." it should read: *"... for You heal without charge."* And in the blessing upon leaving the doctor, instead of: *"Blessed is He Who heals without charge,"* **Rambam** reads: "Blessed is He Who heals the sick." (**Hagahot HaGra,** ad loc.).

10. Rava bar Mechasya said in the name of Rav Chama bar Guria, who said it in the name of Rav: Any illness is better than intestinal illness; any pain is better than heart pain; any twinge is better than a twinge in the heart; any evil is better than an evil wife.

(Shabbat 11a.)

11. It is taught [in a Baraisa]: If a person eats without drinking, his food [becomes] blood, and that leads to intestinal illness. If he eats without [afterwards] walking four cubits [**Rashi**: before sleep], his food rots [**Rashi**: it is not digested to form feces], and that leads to foul odor [**Rashi**: bad breath]. If one eats at a time when he needs to relieve himself, it is like firing an oven without first removing the old ashes, and that leads to an odor of infestation [**Rashi**: his entire body is continually polluted with sweat]. If he bathes in hot water without drinking [hot water], it is like heating an oven on the outside without heating it on the inside [**Rashi**: it is of no benefit]. If he bathes in hot water and does not [afterwards] wash himself off in cold water, it is like iron that was put into the furnace but was not [afterwards] plunged into cold water [Rashi: for (the cold

— 200 —

water) strengthens the iron]. If one bathes without [afterwards] rubbing oneself with oil, it is like putting water on a barrel [Rashi: on the bottom and the sides, with the result that (the water does not go in].

(Ibid. 41a.)

12. Our Sages taught [in a Baraisa]: Before going to a formal meal [Rashi: where it would be embarrassing to have to go out to the bathroom in the middle of the meal] one should walk back and forth ten times, going four cubits each time [*Rashi*: he should pause after each time and check to see if he needs to go to the bathroom]; and some say: four times, going ten cubits each time [*Rashi*: they say this is preferable, for the longer walk brings the feces down through the intestines]. Then he may go to the bathroom, and afterwards go [to the meal] and sit in his place.

(Ibid. 82a)

13. Rav Yehudah bar Chaviva taught: Etrogim [citrons], radishes, and eggs – were it not for their outer peel, would never leave the intestines. [*Rashi*: for they would coagulate and harden and produce constipation. With regard to eggs, the reference is (not to the peel but) to the eggwhite, but since it was discussing citrons and radishes, it used the term "peel" regarding eggs also.]

(Ibid. 108b.)

— 201 —

14. Rabbi Yanai sent to Mar Ukva: "Would the Master please send us some of the eye ointments [compounded by] Mar Shmuel?" He sent in reply: "I shall surely send them, so that you should not consider me stingy. However, this is what Shmuel said: 'Better than all the eye ointments in the world is a drop of cold water [*Rashi*: to put in the eye] in the morning and bathing hands and feet in the evening' [*Rashi*: This, too, brightens the eyes].

(Ibid.)

According to **Aroch,** the correct text is: "... and bathing hands and feet in hot water in the evening."

15. Rav Chiya bar Avin said that Shmuel said: "If a person had his blood let and then became chilled, one should make a large fire [on Shabbat, to warm the room] for him, even in the middle of summer."

[*Rashi* states that this law applies not only to one who has had his blood let, but "all the more so, if someone is ill." However, **Shulchan Aruch (Orach Chaim** 328:18) rules that it applies only to one who has had his blood let.]

For Shmuel they chopped up a fine hardwood chair [*Rashi*: They could not find firewood on the day of bloodletting, and at his command they split a chair of *tidhar,* the most expensive kind (of wood)]. For Rav Yehudah they chopped up a cedarwood table. For Rabbah they chopped up a bench, and Abbaye said to Rabbah: "But the Master is violating the prohibition against wanton destruction of property (*bal tashchit*)!" He replied to him: "For me, the prohibition against wanton destruction of my body takes precedence!"

Rav Yehudah said that Rav said: "[If one does not have enough money to buy shoes,] one should always sell [even] the rafters of his home and [use the money to] buy shoes [*Rashi*: for there is nothing more disgraceful than walking barefoot in the public street]; [but] if he has had his blood let and does not have food to eat, he should [even] sell the shoes on his feet and buy what he needs for the meal [*Rashi*: the meal for recovering from bloodletting]." What are the needs of the meal? Rav said: "meat," but Shmuel said: "wine." Rav said "meat," [because the principle is:] "life replaces life." Shmuel said: "wine,"[because the principle is:] "red replaces red."

(Ibid. 129a.)

16. Shmuel said: If someone washes his face and does not dry it thoroughly, he becomes covered with lesions [*Rashi*: "his face cracks; and I say this refers to a type of boils..."]. What is the remedy? He should wash it often with the water [that remains after the cooking] of *silka* [beets, or possibly: spinach].

(Ibid. 133b-134a.)

17. *"And the clouds return after the rain"* [*Ecclesiastes* 12:2] – this refers to a person's eyesight, which goes away after [much] crying.

Shmuel said: "Until the age of forty, tears are replaced [the body replaces the fluid, and one's eyesight is not reduced]. From [forty] on, they are not replaced."

Rav Nachman said: "Until the age of forty, *kochla* [*Rashi*: a kind of wood that is put into a tube and applied to the eye] improves [eyesight]. From [forty] on, even if he fills [his eye with a *kochla* as thick] as the roller-beam of a loom, it maintains [eyesight] but does not improve it." What is he [Rav Nachman] telling us [*Rashi*: by saying, "even...as the roller-beam of a loom"]? That the thicker the *kochla* is, the better it works.

Rabbi Channina's daughter died. He did not weep for her. His wife said to him: "Is it a chicken that you have removed from your home?" He replied: "[Must I undergo] two [sorrows]: the loss of a child, and blindness?" He held the view cited by Rabbi Yochanan in the name of Rabbi Yossi ben Ketzartah: namely, that there are six kinds of tears, three beneficial and three harmful. Those caused by smoke, by crying, and by the bathroom [*Rashi*: "by the bathroom" means: by suffering] are harmful. Those caused by herbs, by laughing, and by produce [*Rashi*: e.g., the smell of mustard] are beneficial.

(Ibid. 151b-152a.)

18. Shmuel said to Rav Yehudah: "Brilliant one! Open your mouth and let your bread come in! Until forty years [of age], food is best; after forty years, drink is best."

(Ibid. 152a.)

19. Everything that is good for this is bad for that [**Rashi**: Everything that is good for this sickness is bad for that one; what is good for the heart is bad for the eyes or for one of the diseases of some other organ], and [everything] that is bad for that is good for this – except for fresh ginger, long peppers, well-sifted bread, fat meat, and old wine. These are good for the whole body.

(Pesachim 42b.)

20. The Sages taught: If someone is suffering a [life-threatening] attack of ravenous hunger (**bulmus**), he should be fed honey or any kind of sweet food, because honey or any kind of sweet food brighten a person's eyes...Abbaye said: When they taught this [that honey stills hunger], they meant only [if the honey is eaten] after a meal, but before a meal it increases hunger...Rav Nachman said that Shmuel said: If someone is suffering an attack of ravenous hunger, he should be fed extremely fatty meat with honey. Rav Huna the son of Rav Yehoshua said: Also well-sifted flour with honey [is good for this]. Rav Pappa said: Even barley flour with honey. Rabbi Yochanan said: Once I suffered an attack of ravenous hunger, and I ran to the east side of a fig tree and personally fulfilled the verse: *"Wisdom saves the life of those who possess it"* [החכמה תחיה בעליה; *Ecclesiastes* 7:12], for Rav Yosef taught: If someone wishes to taste the taste of figs, he should go to the east side [of the tree, because the figs on that side receive the most sunlight and are therefore the sweetest].

(Yoma 83b.)

21. Honey or any kind of sweet food aggravate a wound.

(Bava Kamma 85a.)

22. Rav Chana Bagdataah said: Dates are warming and filling, they promote elimination, give strength, and do not pamper [*Rashi*: do not cause excessive delicacy of the heart, even though they are sweet]. Rav said: "If one has eaten dates, he must not render halachic rulings" [*Rashi*: because they confuse one's thoughts like intoxication].

[The Gemara objects that Rav's statement about the intoxicating properties of dates is contradicted by the following teaching of the Sages:] "Dates in the morning or evening are beneficial; in the afternoon, harmful; at midday they are incomparable, and they overcome three things: bad thoughts, intestinal disorders, and hemorrhoids."

[*Rashi* explains: The rule is that dates are beneficial after a meal; in the morning people usually eat bread for breakfast...in the evening (the dates are eaten) after dinner; therefore dates are beneficial in the morning or evening. But in the [late] afternoon they are harmful, because they are eaten before the meal, after the midday nap. On the other hand, at midday, right after the meal, when one has eaten his fill and has not yet gone to sleep, they are incomparable, i.e., they are even better than in the evening, since in the daytime one can go into the fields to the outhouse whenever one wishes, whereas at night this is troublesome. "Bad thoughts" means worries; dates at midday overcome them because dates rejoice the heart, and midday is a time of light and rejoicing.]

[The Gemara replies to the foregoing objection:] Did [Rav] say that [dates] are not beneficial? They are certainly beneficial, but they temporarily confuse. This is comparable to wine...

Abbaye said: Mother told me that [eating] dates before bread is [harmful] like a saw to a tree; [but eating them] after bread is [strengthening] like a lock and bolt to a door.

(Ketubot 10b.)

23. It was taught: One who fills his stomach full of anything [*Rashi*: any kind of food that one enjoys, and that is sweet to his palate, and he eats it to the full extent of his appetite] will be afflicted with [the malady called] *ahilu*. Rav Pappa said: "[This applies] even to dates." [The Gemara asks:] Isn't it obvious [that dates are included]? [The answer is:] Since the Master said: "Dates are filling and warming, they promote elimination, give strength, and do not pamper" [*Rashi*: since they are so beneficial to the body], one might have thought that [filling one's stomach with them does] not [cause *ahilu*]. But Rav Pappa informs us that in fact [overeating even of dates causes *ahilu*].

What is *ahilu?* Rabbi Elazar said: "[It is] fire in the bones..." What is the remedy? Abbaye said: Mother said that all the drinks are three, seven, or twelve [*Rashi*:

With every beverage that people drink for healing, there is a fixed number of days during which they must drink it; some must be drunk for three days, some for seven, and some for twelve]; but this [the remedy for **ahilu**, must be drunk] until one is well. All the others [must be drunk] on an empty stomach; but this – after one has eaten and drunk. Then he should go to the bathroom and come out and wash his hands, and he should be brought a handful of **shesita** [**Rashi**: a food made of flour, lentils and salt] and a handful of well-aged wine and these should be mixed together, and he should eat [the **shesita**]. Then he should wrap himself in his sheet [**Rashi**: so that his body will warm up and sweat] and should sleep. No one must wake him until he gets up by himself [**Rashi**: because the sweating is good for him]. When he does wake up, his sheet must be removed from him; for if he does not [remove the sheet, the **ahilu**] will return to him.

(Gittin 70a.)

24. Rabbi Channina said: Why is no one in Babylonia afflicted with **raatan** [**Rashi**: a disease caused by a parasite attached to the brain]? Because they eat **teradin** [beets, or possibly: spinach] and drink **hizmei** beer. Rabbi Yochanan said: Why is no one in Babylonia afflicted with **tzaraas** [leprosy]? Because they eat **teradin,** drink beer, and bathe in the waters of the Euphrates.

(Ketubot 77b.)

25. Rabbi Yochanan proclaimed: Beware of the flies of those afflicted with **raatan!** [**Rashi**: The flies that rest on a person who has **raatan** tend to infect others with the disease.] Rabbi Zeira would not sit in their wind [**Rashi**: in a place where the same wind that blew on the sick person would blow on him]. Rabbi Elazar would not go into the same house with them. Rabbi Ami and Rabbi Asi would not eat eggs from the street where [the sick person] lived. Rabbi Yehoshua ben Levi surrounded himself with them [with **sufferers** from **raatan**] and engaged in Torah-study [**Rashi**: He would attach himself to them while studying Torah and would have them sit next to him, and was confident that the Torah would defend him and he would not be harmed].

(Ibid.)

26. Shmuel said: An encrusted head [**Rashi**: due to not combing one's hair regularly] leads to blindness [**Rashi**: the filth of the head destroys one's eyesight]. Encrusted clothes lead to idiocy [**Rashi**: If one does not wash his clothes regularly, and wears them when they are filthy, this brings him to idiocy and confusion]. An encrusted body [**Rashi**: encrusted with dirt] leads to painful boils.

(Nedarim 81a.)

27. Eliahu told Rabbi Natan: Eat one third, drink one third, and leave one third [**Rashi**: Fill one-third of your stomach with eating, one-third with drinking, and

leave one third of it empty]. Then when you become angry you will be full [**Rashi**: When your stomach is filled with anger, you will be full; but if you fill your stomach with eating and drinking, then when you become angry (the stomach) will split].

Rabbi Chiya taught: If one wishes to avoid intestinal disorders, he should be in the habit of dipping [**Rashi**: dipping his bread in vinegar or wine] summer and winter. If you are enjoying your meal, leave it. And do not delay using the toilet when you need to.

(Gittin 70a.)

28. Rabbi Yochanan said: It would be better to drink a cup of sorcerer['s brew] than to drink a cup of lukewarm [water]. However, this applies only if [the water] is in a metal vessel. If it is in a pottery vessel there is no harm. And even if it is in a metal vessel, it is only if it was not boiled. But if it was boiled there is no harm. And this [that unboiled lukewarm water in a metal vessel is dangerous] applies only if one did not put *tzivi* into it; but if one put *tzivi* into it there is no harm. [**Rashi**: *Tzivi* means anything that one puts into a drink, such as herbs, spices, or fragrant roots.]

(Bava Metzia 29b)

29. The Sages taught: One who has had his blood let should not eat milk, cheese, onions, or cress. If he did eat [any of these, what should he do]? Abbaye said: He should take a *reviis* [about one-half to one cup] of

vinegar and a *reviis* of wine, mix them together, and drink it.

(Avodah Zarah 29a.)

30. Our Sages taught: Six things heal a sick person of his sickness, and their healing is [truly] healing. They are: cabbage; *teradin* [beets, or possibly: spinach]; the water of dry *sissin* [**Rashi**: (The) dry (*sissin*, an herb whose name in Old French is) *foliol* is steeped in water and drunk]; the maw of an animal; the womb of an animal; and the *yoteret al hakaved* [an organ or membrane over the liver]. Some say also small fish. And not only that, but small fish make one's whole body flourish and grow.

Ten things cause a sick person to have a relapse and make his illness severe. They are: eating [the following foods:] beef; fat; roasted meat; fowl; a roasted egg; and cress; having a haircut; going to the bathouse; [eating] cheese; [eating] liver. Some say also [eating] nuts. Some say also [eating] squashes [קישואין; *kishuin*]. The academy of R' Yishmael taught: Why are they called *kishuin*? Because they are as harmful [קשה, *kasheh*] to the entire body as swords.

(Ibid.)

Bach notes that in **Berachos** 57b the list of harmful foods omits liver and has milk in its place. The Gemara there adds that only large squashes are harmful, but small ones are beneficial.

31. Rabbi Yishmael the Great says: The stones on which we sat in our youth waged war upon us in our

old age [they chilled our body and therefore we became weak in our old age]. Rabbi Yonah commanded the scholars: Do not sit on the outer stone benches of the house of study of Bar Ulla, because they are cold. Rav commanded the disciples: Do not sit on the outer stone benches of the house of study of Asi, because they are cold. Rabbi Abbahu went down to bathe in the hot springs of Tiberias. He supported himself on two boards [so as not to get chilled by walking on the stone floor]. They would fall down and he would straighten them up again and again. He was asked: What are these for? He replied: I am guarding my strength for my old age.

(Jerusalem Talmud, Beitzah 1:7, as cited by Otzar Musarei Chazal.)

]32. [It is taught in a Baraisa:] Ten things lead to hemorrhoids. They are: eating bamboo leaves; grape leaves; grape tendrils; the *morigim* of an animal [**Rashi**: any part of the animal's body where the meat is not smooth, but is bumpy or furrowed; e.g., the skin of the tongue] without salt; the backbone of a fish; salted fish that is not fully ready; drinking the dregs of wine; using lime or clay to wipe oneself [after going to the bathroom]; and wiping oneself with a stone that someone else has already used [for the same purpose]. Some say: also suspending oneself [**Rashi**: not sitting down] in the bathroom.

(Shabbat 81a.)

33. Rav Yehudah said: There are three things which, when done at length, bring a person length of days and years: taking a long time in prayer; taking a long time at his meal [*Rashi*: so that the poor will come and receive sustenance]; and taking a long time in the bathroom [*Rashi*: this is healthy].

(Berachos 54b.)

34. Be careful of three things: Do not sit too much, for sitting causes hemorrhoids; do not stand too much, for standing is hard on the heart; and do not walk too much, for walking is hard on the eyes. But spend one-third of the time sitting, one-third standing, and one-third walking.

It is more comfortable to stand than to sit without support. [*Rashi*: For example, on a couch or armchair there is support; on a bench or on a pillow there is no support.]...But you said that standing is hard on the heart! Rather, it is more comfortable to stand with support than to sit without support.

(Ketubot 111a-b.)

INDEX

Key To Scripitural, Talmudic and Midrashic References

WRITINGS

SPELLING AND STYLE

1. Transliteration is Sephardic consonants and vowels: **truth = emet.**
2. Books of Tanach are in Engl. form: **Genesis.**
3. Names are in Heb. form: Yaakov.

A: **Avraham.**

B: **Baal Haturim.**

C: **Chagigah.**

D: **Da'at.**

G: **Gemara; gematria.**

K: **Kehilas Yaakov.**

M: **mo'ach.**

S: **Shabbat. Shem MiShmuel. Shemoneh Esreh** Prayer.

Y: **Yaakov. Yitzchak.**

About the Author

Rabbi Matityahu Glazerson was born and educated in Israel. He studied at Medrashiat Noam in Pardes Chana, and at various yeshivot, including Kfar Chassidim, Ponievez, and Chevron. Today he is involved in teaching in a Kollel, and lecturing in various institutions like Neve Yerushalayim, Ma'ayonot Yerushalayim and Kol B'Rama. He is instrumental in paving a new way toward the instillment of Jewish values. Rabbi Glazerson is the author of many books, including *The Secrets of the Haggadah*, *Music and Kabbalah*, and *Above the Zodiac*.